PRAISE FOR THE ANXIOUS SALESMAN

"Sheldon Snodgrass offers a raw, intimate glimpse into the challenges we all face, and delivers a must-read for those seeking balance, success, and peace in the demanding world of sales."

Steve Giannone, Sales Director, Central
Region Risk Strategies

"Written above and beyond so many other titles in this crowded space, Sheldon Snodgrass blends business wisdom with a folksy, tell-it-like-it-is style that reaches right to the heart of how salespeople can evolve. He seamlessly weaves examples of professional growth with lessons on motivation, habit change, and reducing anxiety. With optimism, metaphor, strategy, and enthusiasm, this book imparts an "I can do it" attitude with practical ways to achieve greater outcomes."

Marsha Kline Pruett, PhD, Professor, Smith College
School for Social Work, Department of Psychology

"Like a favorite movie watched time and again, this book should be on the rotating top shelf of anyone in a high-performance role that requires motivation, inspiration, and dedication."

Jeremy Wilmes, Regional Sales Director,
Cetera Financial Group

"Sheldon Snodgrass has done something no other sales author has ever done: he has exposed the soul of the salesman by channeling the dueling dialogues of his inner coach and inner critic to help readers melt the barriers holding back their success. Read at the risk of being inspired to take bigger personal risks to achieve 10X success."

Charlie Epstein, Actor, Entertainer, and
Founder of The 401k Coach

"This groundbreaking field guide blends witty anecdotes and practical advice to inspire meaningful change among novice and seasoned professionals alike, no matter the industry."

Tory Pachis, Senior Vice President Marketing
& Communications, Amica Insurance

"Where was this manual for me some 37 years ago? Snodgrass touches all bases necessary to find greater calm amidst the pressure to make sales happen."

Timm Marini, President, Western New England,
HUB International New England

"Snodgrass' unique approach, blending analysis with humor, not only entertains but also empowers readers to navigate their professional hurdles effectively."

Aubie Knight, CEO, North Carolina Independent
Insurance Agents Association

THE ANXIOUS SALESMAN

A FIELD GUIDE

How to Transform Your Inner Critic
into a Championship Coach

J. SHELDON SNODGRASS

Published by
McCurdy House Media
mccurdyhousemedia.com
Williamsburg, MA USA & Mexico City, Mexico

ISBN:979-8-9897388-0-9 (Hardback)
ISBN:979-8-9897388-1-6 (Paperback)
ISBN: 979-8-9897388-2-3 (eBook)
ISBN: 979-8-9897388-3-0 (Audio Book)
Library of Congress Control Number: 2023924475

Front cover, interior layout and design by
Seth Gregory, sethgregorydesign.com

Call to mind one person who lifted you
up when you were down.

Remember when you did the same
for someone else.

To the helper in all of us,
and to my Dad, especially.

This field guide will help transform the
noisy chatter of your inner critic into
the uplifting dialogue of a championship
coach who meets you where you are and
fires you up to win the day.

CONTENTS

HOW DO I USE THIS FIELD GUIDE?

1. **Jump in anywhere.**

   The order in which you read this book doesn't matter. Each chapter comprises the same five-part structure that delivers topical lessons to consider and act upon. Take your time. Read no more than one chapter per day.

   The Dilemma: From existential to intrapersonal, you'll identify a vexation that many salespeople share.

   The Takeaway: What the chapter delivers to help you solve the dilemma.

   The Dueling Dialogue: Eavesdrop on a private conversation among three parties wrestling with the dilemma—my inner critic, my inner coach, and my anxious self.

   The Coaching: Designed to trigger your own flash of insight, here you'll unpack the chapter's lessons for yourself and decide if and how to apply them.

   The Next Step: If the chapter's lessons resonate, a three-minute exercise and a three-second affirmation make it clear what to do next to integrate them.

2. **Attune** to how you talk to yourself about your achievements and plans. You'll need to be honest and quiet to do this.

3. **Take just two steps: one inward, one outward.**

   The inward step means simply to notice the chatter—often a screaming match—of your dueling mind. This step requires a quietude I will show you how to access throughout this guide.

   The outward step means right action. Think "right" not in the moral sense (although it could be) but in the manner of a small boat with a heavy keel; it will get knocked about but will always right itself, just as you can.

   That is what this entire book is about: Wresting control from the inner critic, its siren song of rationalizations, justifications, or flagellations so we may connect to the most powerful truth needed in any moment of choice, then choosing—again and again and again.

4. **Repeat. Again.**

   We get 10 billion tries to master this. No lie. Here is the math:

   Professor Andrew Olendzki, the Director of Mindfulness Studies at Lesley University, writes that we have six moments of cognition per second.

That's 360 per minute which equals 21,600 per hour. Assuming 7.5 hours of sleep per day we can have 356,400 mind-moments per waking day.

Over a 77-year-lifespan we may have 10 billion discrete episodes of experience. Think of that as 10 billion do-overs.

WHY CAN I TRUST THIS FIELD GUIDE?

You can trust this field guide because every chapter combines autobiographical insight, distilled from thirty years of sales calls and journal entries, with ancient wisdom and clinical research on peak performance and human potential.

The result is a practical yet profound guide that draws upon my time in the trenches as a soldier, sales rep, sales coach, entrepreneur, and competitive athlete.

I also draw from three well-researched founts in the field of human psychology which any of us can channel as we listen to our inner dialogue. I unwittingly discovered these powerful means to inner wisdom as I wrestled with my own demons.

VOICE DIALOGUE THERAPY

Although I certainly recommend psychotherapy, and it has helped me immensely, I'm now at the point where I recognize most of the players chattering, whispering, or bellowing in my mind's ear. Voice Dialogue Therapy is an integrative modality which helps one understand and converse with distinct parts of one's psyche—something you will witness in the "Dueling Dialogues" of every chapter.

SELF-AFFIRMATION THEORY

I always thought self-affirmations were crap, telling myself I could manifest anything, that I was a success even as I failed, that something would be right when it felt so wrong. Turns out they are crap—unless you use them properly. Self-Affirmation Theory is about speaking potent truths to persistent pains. You will have the opportunity to do that at the end of each chapter. I also included a Do It Yourself (DIY) guide on page 175.

MINDFULNESS MEDITATION

"Who the hell has time to meditate or practice mindfulness?" Many of the wise, compassionate, peaceful, and productive among us. "Yeah, but they don't have the pressure, demands, and woe that I do." Indeed, many of them have much more. Mindfulness Meditation—the practice of presence—is perhaps the single most potent skill in the toolkit of life. Particular chapters in this book invite you to try it.

AND YOU SHOULD KNOW...

I ally with the shared humanity in all of us and I use
the grammatical masculine throughout this book. I
also swear a bit. I mean no offense.

WHY CAN I TRUST THIS AUTHOR?

You can trust me because I've spent decades making many thousands of cold calls, follow up calls, and sales calls. I've crushed quotas and know the peaks of high income, high praise, and high life. I've also been crushed by quotas, been fired four times, and know the depths of doubt, debt, and despair.
I am my own laboratory.

I'm a fourth-generation, airborne-qualified U.S. Army veteran. I'm also an Alpine Certified Level 2 ski instructor and certified white-water river guide who has taught thousands of people how to do both.
I know what it's like to be scared.

I've sold advertising, leadership development programs, econometric impact models, web- design services, corporate-travel services, financial services, consulting services, IT outsourcing, and my own sales coaching seminars.
I know what it means to hunt and be hungry.

I spent a year leading scuba excursions for a start-up in Mexico, another year coaching adjudicated teens in an Outward Bound–style prison program, and another year as a high-ropes instructor in a leadership-training facility.
I know what it means to try, try again.

My ADHD emerged when I was eleven years old and I finally mastered it 40 years later. I've had a regular mindfulness meditation practice for 30 years. I've pursued couples and individual psychotherapy with six different clinicians. I've worked with three sports performance coaches as an adult and I have dedicated my career to keeping other people fired up.
I know what it means to face inner demons.

My adrenaline sports pursuits have left enough scar tissue from lacerations, punctures, tears, breaks, and surgeries to stitch a quilt. I've competed internationally on grand- masters-level ultimate-frisbee teams and have had podium age-group finishes in grueling mountain-trail races. I raced in four triathlons during my inaugural year, won an Olympic-distance state championship in my second year, and in my third year raced against the country's elite in the USA Triathlon Age Group National Championships.
I know what it means to maintain discipline.

I've lived in ten states, four countries, and on two continents, ultimately settling in New England where my wife and I raised two human beings into conscientious and contributing adults. One earned an Ivy League education and the other a Fulbright Scholarship along the way.
I know the jubilation and tribulation of family life.

Though Catholic, I helped my Jewish wife create the first and only Reform Jewish synagogue in Florence, Massachusetts. I also built the local-high-school ultimate-frisbee program including a scratch girls team that became nationally ranked in five years.
I know the power of belief.

And, as if all that had not prepared me for the achievement of a lifetime, I cared for, cried with, caressed, cajoled, cooked and cleaned for, coached, and carried my wife through seven hellish years of her titanic struggle with a brain injury. We celebrated her complete recovery during a five-month sabbatical abroad whereupon I finished this book.
I know love.

And I can still be judgemental, ill-tempered, self-doubting, and clueless.
I know I'm a work in progress.

CHAPTER 0.5

I'VE HEARD
IT ALL BEFORE

We often ignore the truth even
though we don't intend to.

"The future belongs to those who prepare for it today," counsels Malcolm X. "I am the master of my fate," declares William Ernest Henley's poem, "Invictus." "I reap what I sow," teaches Galatians 6:7-8. "Destiny is not a matter of chance, it is a matter of choice," says the poet William Jennings Bryan.

Awesome! Love it. So true. I'm pumped to make some sales calls and have a killer day. I'm just gonna finish this quick YouTube video of epic mountain bike descents before I get back to work.

And that's how we ignore the greatest truths in the tiniest of moments.

The profundity of axioms is also their problem. Because of their unassailable resonance, they appear boundless, so lofty that they become abstractions that turn into whispers easily ignored after a bludgeoning by an inner critic who leaves us anxious, angry, or avoidant.

Another problem with wise words is that we use them to justify contradictory positions.

Sir Winston Churchill admonishes me, "Never give in— never, never, never, never."

But Kenny Rogers sings to me, "Know when to hold 'em. Know when to fold 'em. Know when to walk away. Know when to run."

One minute my inner coach pumps me up to keep making sales calls. In the next, my inner critic spews doubt because I'm not reaching decision makers or closing deals. I think there has to be a better way.

On and on the contradictions roll:

"If not now, when," questions Hillel the Elder. While the poet Violet Fane tells us, "Good things come to those who wait."

"Eat, drink and be merry, for tomorrow we die," says the Mormon Book of Nephi. While the movie classic *Gone With the Wind* ends with "Tomorrow is another day."

Benjamin Franklin warns, "If you fail to prepare, you are preparing to fail!" While Jane Austin's Emma entreats, "How often is happiness destroyed by preparation, foolish preparation!"

Dammit, what's a salesman to do? Take two steps: one inward, one outward. *(See, "How Do I Use This Field Guide," page x.)*

CHAPTER 1

ON ANXIETY

There is no cure for anxiety any more than there is a pill for happiness.

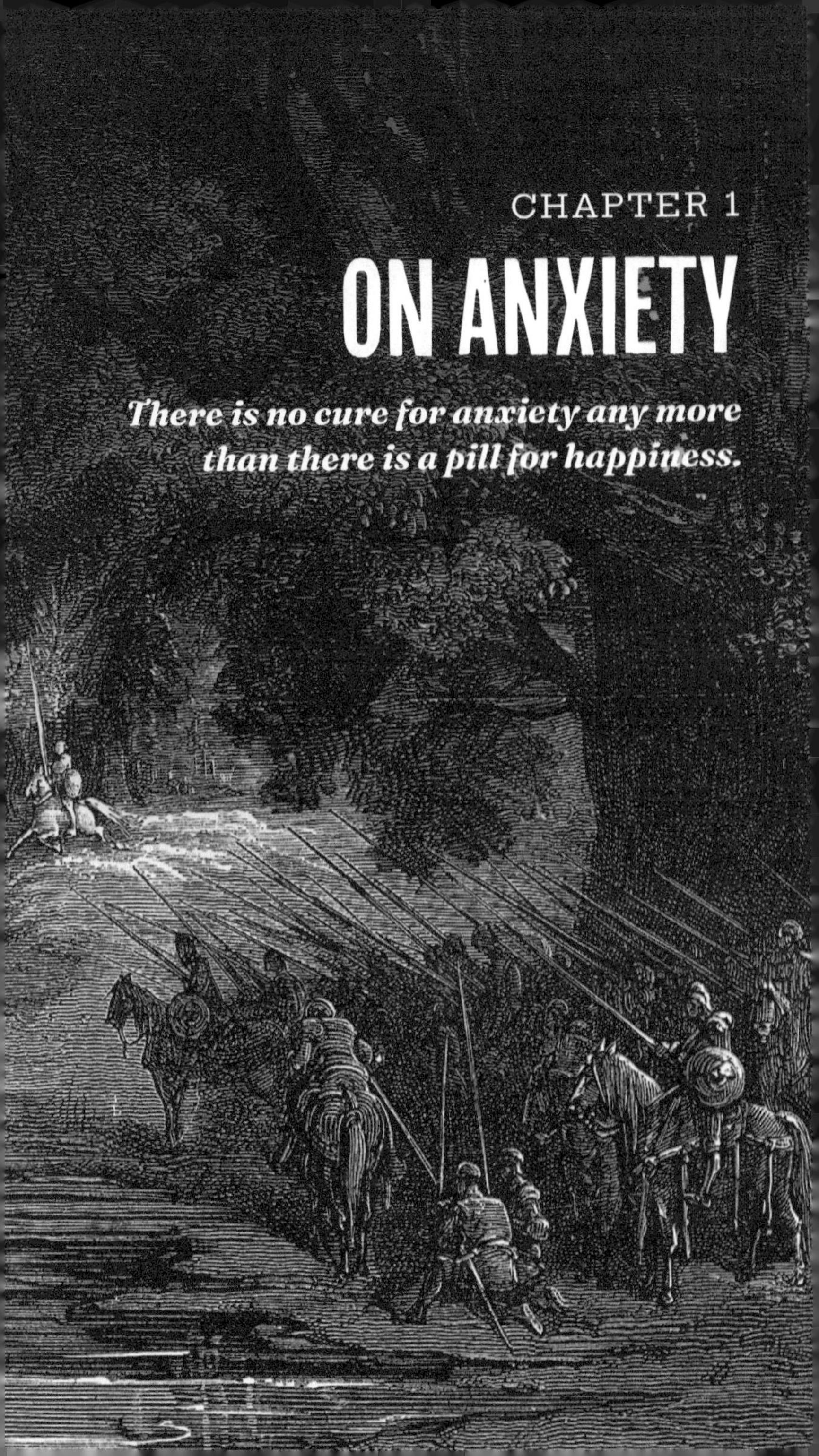

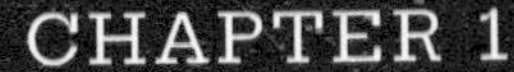

THE DILEMMA

I often feel anxious even when there is nothing obvious to worry about.

There is frequently an accompanying voice that says I'm not good enough or I'll get it wrong or I'll never make it.

I have plenty of concerns about my money, my family, my health, and my work, but dammit, even when those things seem ok there's a semi-constant flutter of tension or nervousness or worry in my chest.

How can I resolve this?

On a scale of 1 to 10, rate the degree to which you find this dilemma reappearing in your life. If it's more than five, reread the coaching and next steps of this chapter three more times in the next month.

| 1 | 2 | 3 | 4 | 5 | 6 | 7 | 8 | 9 | 10 |

THE TAKEAWAY

Read this chapter if you sometimes feel anxious or carry a gnawing sense of agitation or disquiet in your body, or preoccupation in your mind.

You will understand how all of your anxiety derives from one of, or a combination of, just three sources, and then learn a four-step framework to relieve it at any time in any place.

Your anxiety will diminish in frequency and intensity as you learn to distinguish when it is your actions (including avoidance) causing your feelings, or when it is your feelings of anxiety causing your actions.

You will stop seeking the ideal entry point in the feeling/action loop and know that, like entering a circle, everywhere and nowhere is the perfect beginning and end.

It shows up in this dueling dialogue...

THE DUELING DIALOGUE

COACH: Good morning!

Me: Yep, except for this friggin' tension in my chest. Not sure why I have it right now, but it's unpleasant. Kinda like I drank too much coffee or misplaced my wallet, or have to make a speech or something. I don't know.

Critic: I'll tell you why. It's because you didn't wake up early and exercise like you said you would. You feel guilty.

Me: Yeah, but I hit it hard yesterday, and I've been on a great roll with my early morning exercise commitment.

Critic: Excuse! You said you would. You didn't. Now you feel crappy about it.

COACH: Maybe. What did your body tell you today?

Me: To curl up, stay in bed, possibly do some mellow exercise this evening.

Critic: Everybody's body says that! If everybody listened to their first impulse all the time, we'd all be a bunch of non-achieving slackers.

COACH: It's true that our first impulses don't always serve us. Thanks for the warning. It's also true that sometimes we have to listen to our bodies, not our minds. Sometimes both.

Me: How do I know which to listen to,
my body or my mind?

COACH: Be silent.

Me/**Critic**: Huh?

COACH: You have to be still, allow the sensations and mental chatter to wash over and through you. Then an integrated answer will emerge.

Critic: Sounds like a waste of time. Just get it done.

COACH: With or without that gnawing sense of anxiety, tightness in his chest, and that jittery foot?

Critic: I don't care, doesn't matter. Get 'er done.

Me: I've tried that before, 'just getting it done,' and I still felt anxious. Like today, I know I made the right choice, yet I still have this gnawing agitation in my solar plexus. It's like a flutter of nervousness that I can't shake off. It's a real joy suck.

Critic: It's called guilt, you idiot. And you feel it because you slacked off in some other way. You tubed out. You ate crap. You slept in. You procrastinated. You avoided. You smoked weed. Whatever. You should feel guilty!

COACH: So, you are calling his anxiety, guilt?

Critic: I don't care what you call it: guilt, anxiety, shame, tension. It's the feeling that he should be doing something else, something different, something more, something better.

COACH: That is a helpful feeling sometimes. What if he's doing exactly what he should be doing when he should be doing it yet the feeling lingers? What then?

Critic: I don't care. It doesn't matter because he's getting stuff done and the feeling will eventually fade.

Me: Yeah, it fades but it returns often and lingers far too long.

Critic: That's life, man. Deal with it.

COACH: I thought you'd say that. How 'bout we get 'er done with less anxiety?

THE COACHING

For most of my adult life I have awakened feeling anxious. This anxiety carries a gnawing, annoying feeling in my solar plexus or my trapezius. Journal entries since my days as an Army Officer in 1989 confirm an omnipresence of anxiety varying only by degree.

The sensation of anxiety often brings hisses of "You aren't good enough," "You're an imposter, a faker," "You'll be found out," "You'll get it wrong," "You've bitten off more than you can chew," "You'll never make it," "You'll never finish," and other similarly unhelpful rasps.

Often, I have no idea why I'm anxious, even when I take the time to reflect on why. "Yep, money is flowing. Yep, there's no pressing demand on me now. Yep, in this moment all is well with my family, my health, and my work. Dammit, there's that familiar flutter in my chest!"

I used to hate this voice but now I'm better at making friends with it. Well, not a friend so much as a pesky tag-along whom I tolerate because I simply cannot ditch him.

Sometimes this tag-along ruins my day by dragging me into a pit of inner torment about why the hell I can't willpower him away. I'm left with a shaken resolve or an oozing doubt about my business value, my skills, or my future.

Other times I'm grateful that he forces me to look inward where I'll often see a broken promise to myself, a next simple step forward, or the promise of renewed vigor.

The accompanying mental chatter swings from "I am at one with the birds. They don't fret," to thoughts of ending up as a panhandler as I wallow in defeatist self-talk.

Certainly, psychotherapy and medication are important tools in providing relief if one has been diagnosed with an anxiety disorder. But neither therapy nor medication is a panacea. Clinical interventions, be they medical or therapeutic, serve to create more internal and external space from which to act.

It is within this space that one must still do the hard work of managing mindset and behavior, both of which impact the other. Think of prescription medications and therapy performing like a football lineman who creates openings through which a quarterback must still run a play to advance the ball, sometimes for a big gain, other times for a sack.

One step that I typically take to ditch my tag-along is to isolate the source of the anxiety, which always comes from only one of three places or a combination of each. There is often no distinct line between these sources. They can morph and blend into one another, and there are always only three: biological, situational, or existential.

1. The **biological source** means that sleep, nutrition, or exercise (and for some people, medication) will create the space through which I need to move toward calm.

2. The **situational source** means I can point to a trigger for the angst: money is tight, my sales pipeline is weak, I procrastinated or avoided, my surroundings are agitating, a deadline looms, a relationship is troubled, I lied, or I stayed angry.

3. The **existential source** means I can't isolate a single choice but am carrying the weight of accumulated traumas, unhelpful choices, missed marks, or lapses of integrity over many hours, days, or even months. That is, I am feeling the cumulative effect of pain or falling short of my own commitments, best intentions, or desires without forgiving myself. *(See Chapter 5, "On Not Being Good Enough" and Chapter 10, "On Gratitude and Forgiveness.")*

Whether the source of my angst is obvious or mysterious, the best way I have found to ditch this pesky tag-along is a four-part mantra that, ironically, my army drill instructors taught me during my M-16 rifle qualification test: breathe-relax-aim-squeeze.

With a slight modification, here is how I translate this weapon firing maxim into anxiety relief.

1. **Breathe.** This means I fully experience the anxiety. Fighting is futile. I feel it in my body and let it wash over me. Right here, right now it fills me. Resistance doubles my burden because I've added agitation to the angst. I breathe slowly and deeply. I note the anxiety with detached curiosity. It is what it is. I simply name it and know that, like the weather, it will eventually pass.

2. **Relax.** This means I mentally unhook from the anxiety. The sensation doesn't disappear but I move from solely experiencing it, to also observing it. I don't judge the state because it is not me. Rather, I am in a state. I tune into my body and my breathing, and turn my ears toward a more helpful inner voice. I relax my shoulders. I straighten my back. I may touch my heart. I remind myself that I have been here before but I have also been on the opposite shore. Decoupling from the experience creates a small space into which I can aim.

3. **Aim.** This means forgive and thank. Like the rear and front sights on a rifle, forgiveness and gratitude align perfectly when we aim at truth. Forgiveness creates space for a new, healthier possibility. Gratitude allows us to inhabit that space. Forgiveness clears from our view the haze of negative self-talk to reveal the gifts that gratitude presents infinitely. Forgiveness opens the door to freedom; gratitude carries us in. My belly is full and it functions. My fingers work. I have hot water and a clean towel. I can taste chocolate and whiskey. I hear that bird yonder. I am loved. I have resources. *(See Chapter 10, "On Gratitude and Forgiveness.")*

4. **Squeeze.** This means I move. If I breathe, relax, and aim, I can then step toward anything, particularly that thing that makes me anxious—if it is clear to me. The step may be tiny at first: a big glass of water, a healthy snack, a walk, or repeating a mantra, and then I can move toward the cold call, the stage presentation, or the apology.

Breathe. Relax. Aim. Squeeze.

To reiterate:

- Breathe means we embrace the feeling of anxiety, not fight it.
- Relax reminds us we are not the feeling.
- Aim means we pick an object of gratitude and forgiveness simultaneously.
- Squeeze means one step forward.

THE NEXT STEP

1. The next time you feel any degree of anxiety, perhaps even now, **breathe** consciously. Take three slow, deep breaths and fully experience the sensation of anxiety or worry or agitation coursing through your body.

2. Next, **relax** without telling yourself to relax. Just experience the feeling fully and completely and quietly. Say the words,

"I feel: ____
(sensations)

in my ____
(part of body)

...but that feeling is not me. I've felt this way before. I cannot willpower it away."

Straighten your back, relax your jaw, drop your shoulders, and sink into your seat as you continue to breathe in these words:

"This feeling is not me. I've felt this way before. I cannot willpower it away."

This will almost be a meditation.

3. After a minute or two of relaxing, take **aim** with your eyes closed. Put a soft, compassionate smile upon your face.

    See yourself in your mind's eye and say,

    *"I forgive you for*________________________

    ____

    ________________________ *"*

    (Whatever rises to the top of your list of offenses.)

    Next, with your eyes still closed, whisper softly,

    *"I am grateful for*________________________

    ____

    *and*________________________

    ________________________ *"*

    (Fill in both blanks)

4. Finally, take another conscious breath and **squeeze.** With the objects of forgiveness and gratitude still firmly in your mind, decide what you can do in the next nine to ninety-minutes to bring peace to yourself and do it.

AFFIRMATION

Quietly repeat the following affirmation when you find yourself struggling with this chapter's dilemma or write your own using the DIY guide on page 175.

I welcome this challenging feeling as a teacher silently bringing me lessons that I am learning to understand.

MY OWN AFFIRMATION

____

____

____

CHAPTER 2
ON ACCOUNTABILITY
The great deception with accountability is that we mistake it for responsibility and we end up equating our worth with our results.

THE DILEMMA

I secretly hate accountability. I know what my responsibilities are but I don't want to be measured or monitored, so I often avoid it if I can.

I try my best to achieve goals but often get waylaid by people, events, or circumstances outside of my control, yet I still carry the blame for the miss.

If I must accept responsibility for my results then I must be held to account for them. But since I can only influence and not control results or outcomes, how then can I be held accountable for them?

On a scale of 1 to 10, rate the degree to which you find this dilemma reappearing in your life. If it's more than five, reread the coaching and next steps of this chapter three more times in the next month.

| 1 | 2 | 3 | 4 | 5 | 6 | 7 | 8 | 9 | 10 |

THE TAKEAWAY

Read this chapter if you aren't hitting your goals, are struggling to manage competing demands, or are feeling demoralized, lost, or overwhelmed with pressure.

This chapter will help you distinguish the subtle but crucial difference between responsibility and accountability so you can unburden yourself of situations beyond your control and focus on what matters most.

You will build your responsibility muscle by being accountable for your progress, regardless of your pace, using just five power tools that are always at your disposal.

It shows up in this dueling dialogue...

THE DUELING DIALOGUE

Critic: Damn, dude, you are way below your quota.

Me: I don't really have a quota—it's more of a sales target or expectation.

Critic: Who the hell cares what you call it? You aren't selling enough.

Me: Shut up! You're freaking me out. I've closed some sales. And I'm certainly keeping busy.

Critic: Busy with bull crap.

Me: Hey, man, it's gotta get done. And everything takes longer than you think. People don't respond or take forever to reply. I've got emails, proposals, research, contracts, correspondence, staff meetings, conferences, side projects, networking events, and calls. Jeez.

COACH: I hear you brother. My dad calls all that stuff "administrivia." It isn't necessarily trivial, it's got to be managed, but it's not the main event. What would your boss say is your ultimate responsibility?

Me: Closed deals.

COACH: Right on. That's a heavy responsibility, my man. Way to step up!

Critic: Ha! He's hardly steppin' up. Dude is spinning his wheels and is still way off target.

Me: It's true. I'm pretty below where I need to be.

COACH: Let's talk about that. Do you know what you need to hit in terms of new closed business for the rest of this year?

Me: Kind of. I could certainly calculate it. We start the year with a revenue goal but everyone generally falls into a range somewhere between what's marginally acceptable and crushing it.

Critic: See! He doesn't even have a clear goal.

COACH: He has a decent enough sense of it. He could produce a number but big numbers are always hard to manage in the moment.

Me/Critic: Huh?

COACH: I mean you have to break big goals down to small actions you can actually account for. Not "I need $20K in revenue" but "I need to make twenty calls to get ten meetings to get five proposals to close one deal." How's your current opportunity pipeline?

Critic: F'n guy has been talking about the same few prospects over and over since last quarter and he's not closing.

Me: I'm working on it! Plus I have a lot gestating in terms of potential lead sources and networking but it all takes time and I keep getting pulled into, what did you call it, administrivia?

COACH: I hear you, that stuff can suck you in like a blackhole, particularly when you don't have a stronger force to oppose it.

Me: What do you mean?

Critic: He means closing, being accountable for new deals.

COACH: No, I don't. I'm saying he has to create a stronger force that acts against the pull of all that administrivia so that he can actually account for the core function, sales activity.

Critic: That's what I said.

COACH: No, it's not. You said he has to be accountable for closing new business. I'm saying he's responsible for closing new business. That's not the same as being accountable.

Critic: Yeah, it is. Besides, I don't care what you call it. He can't duck accountability for results.

COACH: You keep confusing accountability with responsibility. Responsibility means ownership of results. It sounds like he accepts responsibility for that even though it's hard.

Me: That's true, it's all on me but I'm just not making it happen.

COACH: What would you say are the bare-bones essential tasks of selling? What does the raw essence come down to?

Critic: Closed deals!

COACH: Wrong. That's the end result, the thing he's responsible for. I'm asking how he gets there. What does he actually have to do day in and day out to put the count in accountability?

Me: Jeez, I mean so much. Everything we already talked about, the administrivia as you call it, plus so much more.

COACH: Nope. Keep digging for the core of what you have to do.

Me: Man, I'm not sure what you're getting at. I'm doing so many things. But if you forced me to answer I suppose I would say finding and getting in front of good prospects to pitch.

COACH: Bam! Exactly. And if you get in front of enough prospects favorably and repeatedly, make

small agreements, then follow up like your sales
life depended on it—because it actually does—
you'll find where your daily accountabilities
meet your job responsibility. There must
be your laser focus.

Critic: What! He's just gonna ignore everything else?

COACH: Everything else is alluring and supports
sales excellence but is not the core activity. Think
of it like exercise—do you actually need gear,
accessories, memberships, or outfits to get and
keep your heart rate up?

Me: Are you saying I'm doing the wrong things?

COACH: No. I'm saying you're not accounting for
enough of the right things. Accountability
means you count the inputs, the daily doings,
not the output for which you are responsible.
Accountability is about defining your path to a
particular outcome, in this case, low revenue. *(See
Chapter 4, "On Success and Failure.")*

Critic: That's what I've been saying. And
he's way off course.

COACH: Nope. But most people would agree with you.
I think of responsibility as the ability to respond
to results. Accountability is the way we get
there—the things we do to get to the results. Track
those things and you'll strengthen your ability to

respond to how you arrived: win or lose, yes or no, weak or strong.

Me: In this case, my response is "I need some help!"

COACH: Man, don't we all. Grab a pen, your calendar, and your watch. We've got to schedule the rest of your week.

THE COACHING

Listen to the first post-game or post-race questions from family, friends, and fans of any athlete, especially kids. You will always hear, "Who won? What was the score? Where did you place?" Either that or the first thing an athlete will report is a metric.

We justify our focus on scores the way we justify consuming news headlines. "I do it to stay informed," we proclaim. Yet an endless and repetitive cycle of news rarely enhances our understanding of an issue or alters our civic behavior. Instead, we mostly confirm our biases or sour our mood.

Being score focused in pursuit of better performance leaves us as unenlightened as our consumption of headlines in our pursuit of knowledge.

Certainly, news briefs, like score sheets, can be useful. But headlines and race or game results only reveal a glimpse of what we think we need. Final scores give no insight to what matters most about our performance: the path to get there, the effort expended, and the lessons to next apply on our growth journey.

We mostly pay lip service to the more substantive and enduring questions about our pursuits such as, "How was the experience for me? What did I learn? What could I have changed? How does this compare to my personal best? What was a highlight moment? What was hardest? Why?"

Imagine asking those questions to children every time they came off of the soccer field, instead of "Did you win?"

When I compete in races I consciously resist the urge to rush to the scoring table to review my result. "What was my place? How did I do in my age bracket? What was my time?"

I always want those answers and they are fun to get but they are fleeting and misleading, just like sales results.

The best place to assess performance isn't at the end of any pursuit where we have no control over outcomes but throughout the experience of getting there, the journey, as it were—for that is where accountabilities lie. That is where we influence the outcome.

We need only five basic tools for the trip:

1. **A goal.** It doesn't matter what you call it, in the context of any performance journey we need a destination, a target, an objective, an aspiration, something that can give us purpose or direction and can ignite our desire to act in the near term (hours) or the long term (years). But ignition is

precisely that—a start. More is needed to keep any flame alive. The beautiful thing about goals is that they can morph into deadlines.

2. **A deadline.** Be it a due date or a time limit, deadlines have the miraculous ability to keep us on track and they work their magic in any increment. I often set a timer for 30 minutes to help constrain my ADHD monkey mind when I set about a desk task.

   At the other extreme, I have an entire season of trail races and triathlon race dates blocked on my calendar. The beautiful thing about a deadline is that it can morph into a schedule. *(See Chapter 8, "On Finding Flow Amidst Your ADHD.")*

3. **A schedule.** Whether I use a calendar or a clock, a schedule gives me waypoints against which I can measure my core activity and put teeth into the axiom, "What gets measured gets done."

   A schedule is clear, it's trackable and can be as empty or as full as I want to make it. Thus, it functions more like a corral than a cage; it keeps us where we belong but offers plenty room to maneuver. And that maneuver is an endless balancing act between two poles of equal importance, ease and rigor.

4. **Balance.** This is the holy grail. Balance is that often elusive, sometimes confounding, and always necessary part of any performance pursuit. Finding balance forces us to ask questions like:

   - How often and how long must I tilt toward the extreme end of effort, fortitude and rigor, or the opposite direction toward relaxation, spaciousness, and ease?

   - Do I hold fast to a deadline or forgive it?

   - Do I force myself out of bed or sleep in?

   - Do I reprimand or forgive, gut it out or give in, stick to the schedule or remain flexible, or drive on or pause? *(See Chapter 9, "On Sucking It Up.")*

   The answers always come back to balance. Buddha called it the middle way. To help us maintain balance we need support.

5. **Support.** Be they people, places, or things, support for any pursuit comes in many forms. If I am lucky enough to have teammates or a friend on my quest then I have willing accountability partners for the trip. I simply need to treat them as such.

   If it's a solo journey then I find support from rituals, objects, or my environment. This could be looking at a photograph, going for a walk, visiting a library, reciting an affirmation, spending time in meditation, or sitting at a café—anything that buoys my resolve, reanimates my thinking, or centers my mind.

Simply telling someone they must be accountable provides no lift. It's like telling someone they should be nice; it's easy to do when the going is easy. What if I'm exhausted, pissed, late, hungry, or hurt? The best advice then isn't to be nice; it's to take a nap, take a break, take a bite, or take a breath. One can account for those actions far more easily than a mood.

Accountability is similar in that it's easiest when we are on target, in rhythm, and feeling strong, focused, and fulfilled. But that's not when we need accountability the most; we need it when we are demoralized, confused, tired, below quota, scared, or lost. It is then that we have to integrate one or all five of the tools from our kit.

The key to integration is documentation. By whatever means, in whatever format: track, report, reflect, and review. The palest ink, as the old Chinese proverb reminds, is more powerful than the strongest memory.

I have long chronicled my journey toward reduced anxiety, quicker recovery from low production, and a deeper belief in my professional path. I have hundreds of journal entries oozing with recrimination, self-doubt, and failed intentions. I also have hundreds brimming with optimism, strength, and victory.

Here is a journal entry that captures the beautiful synchronization of all five accountability tools during a time of severe anxiety and struggling production.

10/30/2006. I felt in my power this week. A solid A+, the first since I began a tracking process just over 5 months ago. First, let me answer the chipmunk sounding critic. No, I didn't track time all day every day but I tracked a bunch. No, I didn't have my executive planning session last Friday. I'm doing it now, Monday morning. I didn't reexamine my goal focus every morning but I did it at least once during the day. I'm reaping the benefits of this process of self-reflection and goal setting.

I feel the growth of good habits—no trash video, no screen scrolling, and dare I say, no anxiety this week. My frequent lapses of attention, focus, follow through, or commitment are less severe and the aftermath from a slip up is short lived. I'm easily forgiving myself.

My big goal this week was speech prep for my 11/9 presentation and where I might normally feel mounting anxiety, I felt power. I recalled my Uncle Kelley's advice about delivering the best of myself from a place of caring, knowledge, and excitement. It's not about my performance, but my connection. He had me raise my outspread arms and shout, 'I'm terrific. I help people!' Man, that was helpful.

That is victory. That is the result of holistic accountability using all five tools.

THE NEXT STEP

1. Be it analog or digital, your goals, deadlines, and schedules should be written.

    Using whatever medium suits you best, with whatever level of detail feels right, start or keep writing. On a scale of one to ten, rate your current goal writing routine with ten being highest.

| 1 | 2 | 3 | 4 | 5 | 6 | 7 | 8 | 9 | 10 |

2. Don't bog down picking the right tool, the best method, or the optimal process. Stick with what you're naturally drawn to or use any of the the free tools you'll find at SteadySales.com.

    If you rated yourself any number below seven, complete this sentence to advance toward ten:

    During the next five days I will ___________________

    ____

    ____

    ____

3. Review the five-tool accountability list in this chapter and identify your achilles heel, that area where you most struggle with accountability. Write it here:

    ____

    ____

    ____

    ____

4. With this one tool in mind, consider how you might add any level of structure to your day or week—less is more—to support its use.

    For example, "I will practice setting 30-minute timers for myself throughout the day every Monday, Wednesday, and Friday." Write it here:

    ____

    ____

    ____

    ____

5. And stacking tool upon tool, what simple mechanism can you employ to assure you follow through on what you just wrote. Think of this as your support mechanism.

For example, "I will tell my partner what I wrote above and ask her to check in with me at the end of the week." Write it here:

____

____

____

____

This process, though it will ebb and flow and change, should never end. Ever.

AFFIRMATION

Quietly repeat the following affirmation when you find yourself struggling with this chapter's dilemma or write your own using the DIY guide on page 175.

I know that I am the heir to all my actions and therefore welcome the harvest of whatever seeds I sow.

MY OWN AFFIRMATION

____

____

____

____

CHAPTER 3

ON FAILED INTENTIONS

How we stall, why we stall, and when we stall, pale in comparison to the question of how we reset.

THE DILEMMA

I often criticize myself for having a string of false starts, failed intentions, projects in process, and broken promises to myself.

If completion is power, it's no wonder I feel so damn lame about what I've accomplished.

It feels like I only fantasize about big goals or settle for little more than what I'm currently doing or what I have.

How can I resolve this?

On a scale of 1 to 10, rate the degree to which you find this dilemma reappearing in your life. If it's more than five, reread the coaching and next steps of this chapter three more times in the next month.

| 1 | 2 | 3 | 4 | 5 | 6 | 7 | 8 | 9 | 10 |

THE TAKEAWAY

Read this chapter if you look upon your long list of incompletes, missed deadlines, or unfinished plans with self-recrimination, impatience, or regret.

This chapter delivers a powerful, four-step method to find satisfaction with the pace or status of your projects, and puts a new spin on productivity.

You will learn to get comfortable with many starts and few finishes. You will be at peace with initiating and dabbling, knowing that you grow as much from frequent starts as you do from infrequent finishes.

How we stall, why we stall, when we stall are important questions to ask to gain life-enhancing insights but pale in comparison to the question of how we reset.

It shows up in this dueling dialogue…

THE DUELING DIALOGUE

Me: I could have done so much more this hour—all day, really. Hell, all year.

Critic: No joke. So lame.

Me: Well, I did accomplish a few things but not enough. And much of what I started I didn't finish. Mostly, I ignored many of my goals and ideas. Always the same.

Critic: Yep, and here we go again—that knot in your chest, that pit in your stomach, that frenzied and unfocused mind not sure where to start amidst all your oughta dos, wanna dos, and should dos.

COACH: Does it matter how many times he starts and stops?

Critic: Hell yes! It's inefficient and ineffective. Plus he's got a laundry list of incompletes.

Me: That's all true and it makes me nuts. I feel horrible about it.

Critic: It should make you nuts. I'm going to add a nagging sense of guilt combined with agitation as you attempt to make up for all this lost time.

COACH: That can be helpful sometimes, the fire in the belly, the desire to make up for lost time.

Me: Yeah, but my problem is getting out of the productivity pit. I know the way out is with focused completion but I can't gain purchase on any ledge. I try and try again to willpower myself up this wall but feel more self-loathing than I do accomplishment.

Critic: You should feel bad. You're not finishing.

COACH: So, you've added emotional distress to his intentions. Does that help? Are you getting it done now?

Me: No. Well, some days, sometimes I am.

COACH: On those days when you make progress, how do you feel?

Me: Like it isn't good enough, or fast enough. Or like it's too late so I shouldn't even bother.

Critic: That's because it's been dragging on forever. I can't tell you how many times he said it's going to be different next time but it isn't. How he said he would follow through but didn't.

COACH: How else do you feel?

Me: Glad that I started something new or made a little progress on something old.

COACH: So you're sitting with both experiences when you think about your intention—you are pleased with the start or progress but dogged that it's too late or too little. Do I have that right?

Me: Yeah, that's pretty much it. Unless there is absolutely no progress in which case the unmet goal just throbs like irritating background noise.

COACH: What if you focused on your first experience glad that you started?

Critic: Are you kidding me? The world would pass him by! He has a pile of unmet goals. Everybody would be getting things done except him.

COACH: Is anyone keeping score? Is anyone racing against him?

Me: No, but I am.

COACH: Racing against them?

Me: No, just myself, my own standards of performance, what I know is possible.

COACH: So my question remains—what would happen if you concentrated on your first experience of progress—the start and pleasure in the process— as opposed to your second experience of being dogged by incompletion?

Critic: Everything would take forever and nothing would get done.

COACH: I'm asking about his experience of starting something or working towards completion not what he actually completes. Also, is it really everything that would take forever and nothing would get done?

Me: Nah, that's an exaggeration. Some things would get done, some things would drag on but eventually get done, and truthfully some things would never get done.

COACH: You still haven't answered my question. What would happen if you concentrated on your first experience of progress—pleasure in the process— knowing you'll always have only the three possible outcomes you just described?

Me: You mean some things getting done, some things getting done slowly, and some things never getting done? I suppose I wouldn't feel so crappy about what I do or don't complete.

COACH: I like the sound of that!

THE COACHING

I've got goals. I've got projects. I've got persistent intentions to go big or go long. I've also got demands and distractions. I tidy. I dabble. I react. Easily rationalized, such tiny time-sieves can occupy a disproportionate space in my day, particularly when there are no pressing deadlines or deliverables to force my hand.

I can finish the day, even a week, heck, months sometimes, sputtering. That is, my self-imposed commitments soften, a deadline loosens, and progress toward that thing I said is important slips further away.

The tyranny of the urgent or the pull of the petty holds sway. Sure, I may have touched something of strategic importance. I might have inched along. But looking back, I see mostly well-managed minutia instead of a decisive stride forward.

Sometimes the sputter or stall toward the worthier or weightier pursuit is justifiable. Too often though, it isn't. Sometimes becomes oftentimes, oftentimes becomes a year, and a year becomes a decade of woulda, coulda, shoulda, if onlys and didn'ts.

Delays, avoidance, distraction, procrastination, misses, and stalls, while different in many respects, have three elemental truths in common:

- They are inevitable.

- They force resets.

- They leave debris.

If stalls are inevitable that means they are unavoidable. If they are unavoidable that means they should be received as expected and not resented as unwelcome (even though they are).

If we expect something, we adjust for its presence: a highway closure, inclement weather, surgery, bad news. You may still curse it a bit but not with the same force as if it had appeared unannounced. Forewarned is forearmed after all, thus we don't linger as long or as bitterly in our resentment of delay.

How we stall, why we stall and when we stall are important questions to gain life-enhancing insights but pale in comparison to the question of how we reset.

For it is how we start anew that determines the content and size of the debris field we create and walk. Is the field littered with the bitter shrapnel of self-criticism for failed resolve or patient admonitions to try, try again? *(See Chapter 10, "On Gratitude and Forgiveness.")*

The goal deferred or missed entirely isn't, in and of itself, the main problem—although it can be problematic. The more insidious sabotage to completion comes from the monologues that define the debris field of our misses with self-fulfilling prophecies like:

You never finish anything...

Things always take you forever...

You'll flake out on this like you do everything else...

Don't even bother...

Such debris snuffs our inner fire at the very moment we need reignition.

Think of reignition as a reset or personal do over to which we are entitled an infinite number of times until we get it right.

When I think about personal resets I think about how I coach athletes to reset a busted play, a broken rhythm, or a loss of any sort.

Essentially, four things happen. Think of them as the 4Rs:

1. **Reframe**

2. **Readjust**

3. **Recommit**

4. **Repeat**

Depending on the circumstance, the only change to these four elements is the timeframe. Sometimes this four-part process happens in split seconds or minutes, like when a sales opportunity suddenly goes south.

Other times, say completing a book or getting fit, the 4Rs may take days or months or years. For some of us, it may take a lifetime.

Here is a snippet of the mental chatter that replayed countless times during the writing of this book and how I applied the 4Rs.

Damn! I haven't shown much daily, hell, even monthly discipline over the last ten years of trying to finish this book. It's been nagging at me forever. I'm so lame.

Reframe: *"How lucky that I have space to write and get to include so many new lessons that I wasn't ready to teach ten years ago."*

Readjust: *"I'm not going to focus on high-quality writing every day or week. I commit to writing badly at least once a week for any duration."*

Recommit: *"I don't need to finish my book anytime soon. I need to open the file and chip away today."*

Repeat: *"It's actually so much easier to write badly than it is to write well. I think I'll do it again tomorrow."*

Here's how the 4Rs unfurled in mere minutes as I watched myself getting fired halfway through an engagement with a lucrative client.

Reframe: *"Oh, my God, I think they're getting ready to fire me! That's $3K a month gone. Where did I screw up? Be chill, dude. Don't get desperate or defensive. Learn!"*

Readjust: *"Listen and ask questions. Seek first to understand. Discover how we went off the rails after a great six month run—then speak. Focus on the relationship not the revenue."*

Recommit: *"Their requests and expectations aren't realistic but that doesn't make them wrong. Explain my coaching convictions, own my shortcomings but don't grovel. Keep doors open but prepare to let them go."*

Repeat: *"I'll let them breathe for a few weeks and then follow up with a new approach to their old problem. I've been here before. I'll be fine, even if I can't win them back."*

Reframing is a beautiful thing. Unfortunately, it is maligned by our inner critic as dodging accountability or rationalizing poor performance. *(See Chapter 4, "On*

Success and Failure.") Sophisticated thinkers, however, recognize the reframe as a critical component to problem-solving.

Indeed, reframing is the first pillar in the science of design thinking: that elegant, non-linear, iterative approach to making things better.

Another way to think about the reframe is to release an old narrative. For example:

- *"I'm not getting in front of enough prospects and cold calling never works"* becomes *"I have the skills to create a more compelling approach and maintain greater follow up discipline."*

- *"I always feel like I'm barely squeaking by financially"* becomes *"How I earn and spend money is full of opportunity for improvement."*

- *"I'm so constantly buried in sales administrivia that I don't have time for real sales activity"* becomes *"I can delegate, dump, or prioritize my low ROI activities."*

- *"I always fail at my diet and exercise plans"* becomes *"Each day is another chance to start over and experiment with tools for support."*

Readjustment means deciding anew without denigrating. When we have options we can pause, quit, start over, take a baby step, or plunge headfirst again. Readjustment is difficult when the project, the goal, or the idea, that thing we want to complete, torments us for lack of completion instead of soothes us as a work in progress.

Recommitment is possible when we readjust without rebuke. Actually, we can readjust and recommit with a rebuke but it's far less pleasurable. Scold yourself if you must but recommitment to a next step forward is always more powerful when we reframe the problem with curiosity and then readjust our next step with insight.

Repeat. Oh yeah, you are an endless cycle. That's ok. Welcome to life.

One of the best coaches I've ever worked with, Joseph DiCenso, an executive and personal performance coach, once asked me, "If you thought of yourself as a quick starter and a long finisher, how would that change your experience of incompletion?"

Then, adding reframe atop reframe he went on to ask, "If you thought of yourself as a taster of many flavors instead of a connoisseur of a few, how would that change the frustration you feel with so many starts and stops?" Brilliant!

The reset is not the same as rationalizing a long history of woulda, coulda, shoulda, or if onlys.

The reset acknowledges our work in progress the way we might approach a complicated jigsaw puzzle—some pieces are easier than others, some days we make huge strides, other days we dabble or skip entirely.

With a strong reset, never will we stare at our work in progress disappointed we didn't finish today.

THE NEXT STEP

1. Think of any project, goal, or desire that you have long conceived of or struggled to complete. Write one sentence that your inner critic would use to define your efforts or your progress.

   ____

   ____

   ____

2. Read the sentence aloud with a demeaning scoff to your tone of voice.

3. Now think of yourself as a loving, veteran coach, admonishing the critic you just witnessed hissing those words into the ear of a young child.

4. Conjure an image of that coach as yourself and write what you would say to that scoffing, critical adult.

   ____

   ____

   ____

5. Next, reframe your original sentence. Write from the perspective of the veteran coach who reframes your original scoffing sentence in a way that inspires an action step.

    ____

    ____

    ____

6. Read your reframed sentence aloud but this time with the voice of encouragement, love, and support.

    (Criticism is easy, thin, and dismissive. Coaching doesn't deny an outcome, it inspires the next step. Consequently, your reframed sentence must enable you to approach your original project, goal, or desire with an action, including, quite possibly, an indefinite hold.)

7. In thinking about your project, what next step could you take? What clear, next action emerged? Write it here. If nothing revealed itself, try another reframe until your next step is clear.

    ____

    ____

    ____

AFFIRMATION

Quietly repeat the following affirmation when you find yourself struggling with this chapter's dilemma or write your own using the DIY guide on page 175.

I patiently tend the seeds of my garden.
I do not dig them up to see how fast they are growing.

MY OWN AFFIRMATION

____

____

____

____

ON SUCCESS AND FAILURE

Our great folly is that we allow our results, instead of our process to achieve results, to shape our experience of self.

THE DILEMMA

Am I a success or a failure?

I mostly think of myself as successful. I want to believe I'm successful, but I experience failure of will, failed intentions, or failed attempts so often that I'm not sure it's true.

Plus, I hate that my emotional state always seems tied to outcomes I can't control, like reaching prospects, closing deals, or other people's efforts.

I'm not as rich as I want to be, I'm not as fit as I want to be, I'm not as joyful as I want to be.

How can I resolve this?

On a scale of 1 to 10, rate the degree to which you find this dilemma reappearing in your life. If it's more than five, reread the coaching and next steps of this chapter three more times in the next month.

1	2	3	4	5	6	7	8	9	10

THE TAKEAWAY

Read this chapter if you are in a sales slump or feel like you are failing or struggle with a sense that you don't measure up as much as you should.

This chapter will help you decouple your feeling of failure about any outcome in life from the actual failure to achieve it.

No matter what result you seek, you can experience an unassailable feeling of success that isn't delusional or a rationalization even if you don't achieve your intended result.

Learn how to maintain the highest possible standards while escaping the tyranny of the success-failure binary.

It shows up in this dueling dialogue...

THE DUELING DIALOGUES

Me: Ugh, I hate this feeling. Thank God all the definitions of success I've ever read expand way beyond my personal production.

Critic: Duh! You love them because they don't say anything about your actual job. Read the dictionary dude, success is about achieving aims.

Me: I suppose. But it feels so, I don't know, endless and crappy to constantly be defining my success by my results, particularly when I come up short.

Critic: It's crappy because you failed. You went out to close a deal and came back empty handed. That's not success.

Me: But I got some good feedback and some ideas about what I'd do differently next time.

Critic: Ummm, yep, but you failed to close. And this isn't the first time. Don't dance around that word. Admit it, you failed.

Me: Ok, I failed to make the sale but that doesn't make me a failure. I can't be expected to close every time.

Critic: No kidding, but you are way behind, your sales pipeline is thin and people are watching. And this opportunity was huge.

Me: You're making me feel worse. I can't control why this deal didn't close. Besides, I got some value out of the experience.

Critic: Quit trying to find a way around the one definition of success that matters—closed business. Yeah, yeah, you can call yourself successful if you have warm relationships, you learn, you try hard, you're honest and earnest and blah, blah, blah. Dammit, what I'm asking you now is did you close a deal?

Me: No, but I did manage to …

Critic: Shut up. What good are all those things when the deal didn't close? The bottom line is you were hired for a specific purpose. That needs to be your definition of success—closed business!

COACH: Can I jump in here?

Me: Yes! CRITIC: No!

COACH: Let me ask you, Critic, if he had closed the sale would he then be a success?

Critic: Of course!

COACH: And if he closed another one after that? And again and again?

Critic: For sure. He would be a success.

COACH: What if afterward he had a string of losses, what would he then be, a success or a failure?

Critic: That depends on when you ask.

COACH: Oh. So it can change from month to month or day to day. What about hour to hour or minute to minute?

Critic: Uh ... Yeah, I suppose. What's your point?

COACH: I'm trying to understand the value of your labels when their accuracy and applicability is so fleeting and fraught. Why is it so important for you?

Critic: I'm just sick of him trying to duck accountability by dressing up his failures and not taking responsibility for his results.

COACH: How does one get the results you seek?

Critic: Are you kidding me? Tons of stuff! Prospecting! Prepping! Pitching! Follow up, everything! Heck, even those tasks have subtasks that lead to results.

COACH: Then isn't that where we should apply the labels you insist upon, to a process of activity? I mean, to putting one foot in front of the other?

Me: I'm down with that!

THE COACHING

Success or failure appear in any moment as both an emotional experience and an outcome simultaneously.

Our great misfortune is that we confuse the caboose for the engine; forever hitching our emotional sense of efficacy to a final result instead of the efforts we made to attain it, as well as our intentions along the way.

We allow our results, instead of our process to achieve results, to shape our experience of self.

Succeed and you may feel like a success. Until when? Fail and you may feel like a failure. Until when?

It is logical and right that our outcomes should influence our emotions. Our folly is in the outsized influence we ascribe to that linkage, so much so that we mistake influence for cause.

At the level of our unique experience, what matters more, our emotional state or our score? You might argue, convincingly, that without any achievement any feeling of success would be delusional. You would further insist that results, in the end, are what really matter—not intentions, not efforts, not lessons learned.

Your logic falls apart, however, when you consider first that we actually have scant control over outcomes, and second, that one's feeling of success can be inevitable no matter the goal if one stays accountable to the wholesome process of attainment. That is, intention, effort, and evolution. *(See Chapter 2, "On Accountability.")*

It isn't success that breeds success but a feeling of success. And this feeling can emerge at any point in any process circling back upon itself to breed. Sadly, the same is true of failure.

Remarkably, success and failure each contain two identical interior components regardless of exterior results—an emotional experience and a concomitant readiness to act. Our heart either races or retreats and our feet follow suit.

Although our actions unequivocally shape our results, successes and failures stoking or stanching the fires of our experience, we must be alert to how deep and how long we linger with them, and how much we pin our identity to them.

From this process of observation we can draw sustenance, not the product. The question thus becomes not how do we unhinge our experience from our results but how deeply, long, and often we let our results define us.

Success is right here right now. No, it's not. It's over there where the accolade, the goal, or big commission is waiting. Ok, if success is not right here right now but over there where the outcome beckons, what does that make you now, a success or a failure? Do you see the recklessness of such a question, let alone the label?

If you hit your target you are a hero for that period. Then what? Then you are back on the seesaw of defining your success by your production instead of your process.

It is only in the process, that domain of choice making, where you can exert influence on, not control over, outcomes.

You can do everything right, exhibit profound discipline, have clear intent, yet still not win the sale, the game, or the race, or the next one or the next. Does this make you a failure? It is a false binary impossible to resolve except with myopia. We want to resolve it. We feel compelled to resolve it but the success-failure question is specious. We are not one or the other.

Success and failure animate the before, during, and after of any pursuit, they don't define it. Process is the place to make our assessment of success, not production.

It is the feeling of success or failure that is preeminent not the achievement itself. Outcome focus gives you no such option. It is binary. Process focus, on the other hand, is limitless.

THE NEXT STEP

1. Look into a mirror or your mobile phone in selfie-mode and stare at yourself for ten seconds.

2. Say, "I am a successful salesperson." And listen immediately to what your quiet inner voice says in reply. (Substitute a different role if you're wrestling in another domain, perhaps, as a spouse or parent.)

3. Whatever your inner voice says next, ask "Why?"

4. Repeat step three in response to whatever answer you give to "Why?"

5. Repeat step three again and again until you hear a clear next action that results in a "yes" to item two.

   ❈ If you started with a "yes" in item two, ask, "How can I pay this forward by helping someone else?"

6. Bonus:

   ❈ The next time you, a friend, or family member competes in any event, notice if your curiosity is about the outcome instead of the experience. That is a natural urge worth postponing.

※ Instead of first asking about the result, ask about one highlight from the experience and one lesson from the journey to get there. You'll find this a far more generative conversation than one with a binary answer.

AFFIRMATION

Quietly repeat the following affirmation when you find yourself struggling with this chapter's dilemma or write your own using the DIY guide on page 175.

*I ride the waves of my self-observation knowing that,
like a feather on the sea,*

*I am more than what is visible from the peaks
or the valleys.*

MY OWN AFFIRMATION

____

____

____

____

ON NOT BEING GOOD ENOUGH

"Comparison is the thief of joy."

THE DILEMMA

Where is the dividing line between permission to be as I am in any given moment and rationalizing my low performance?

The voice of my conscience and the voice of my critic are scarcely indistinguishable.

How do I maintain a life of high standards without feeling like I'm not measuring up or could always do better or more?

On a scale of 1 to 10, rate the degree to which you find this dilemma reappearing in your life. If it's more than five, reread the coaching and next steps of this chapter three more times in the next month.

1	2	3	4	5	6	7	8	9	10

THE TAKEAWAY

Read this chapter if you sometimes feel like you aren't good enough—your efforts, your performance, your attitude, your results—in comparison to someone or something else.

This chapter separates what you are capable of in any moment from what you deliver in every moment.

See how your constant self-critiques, camouflaged as high standards, hinder instead of help your pursuits.

This will get you off the merry-go-round of self-comparison so you can stop the endless cycle of trying to measure up while feeling like "I'm not enough."

It shows up in this dueling dialogue…

THE DUELING DIALOGUE

COACH: Hey, nice job this week!

Me: Thanks but I could have done a lot more.

COACH: All of us could always do more.

Me: Yeah, but I'm not talking about heroic effort, I just didn't push the way I know that I could have. And today I avoided my early morning prospecting and outreach routine again.

Critic: You better not coddle him. He said he'd hit it early today. He didn't. Don't try to make it ok because it's a pattern like so many others.

COACH: You say that a lot—that he failed or didn't do enough or could have done better or more. He's had some good results with his early start routine.

Critic: Excuse! He said he would. He didn't. Quit making it ok.

Me: It's true. I could have muscled through. I could have gotten up early, made the new calls, finished my follow up, and created more mental space by getting it done.

COACH: And how do you feel about that now, that you didn't start your day the way you wanted to?

Critic: It feels like a pattern. Patterns become pictures. And he's painting a picture of mediocrity.

COACH: Don't interrupt. I'm asking him. How does it feel that you didn't muscle through, get up, get after it, make the calls, clear the ticklers, the whole shebang?

Me: Crappy, confounding, like I don't measure up. It depends on what it is and how I think about it. Generally it feels like a mosquito buzzing in my ear.

COACH: That's maddening. I'm sorry.

Critic: That's the voice of his conscience you weenie, not a mosquito!

COACH: It could be his conscience. Or it could be your voice that's buzzing in his ear. Does this feeling occur only when you fall short of this particular intention?

Me: Heck no. I feel this way too often. It comes up when I race, when I train, when I sell, when I work, when I do just about anything that takes effort or discipline or follow-through. Especially if I see other people crushing it.

COACH: What does that voice say?

Critic: I already told you! He could have done better or more. He fell short. He didn't go big enough or long enough or hard enough. He wasn't optimized. He wasn't as disciplined or focused as he could have been compared to all those high achievers.

COACH: Why are you so unrelenting and comparative, even in the face of small wins or good performances or strong efforts?

Critic: Because if I let up, he'll founder. He already slacks off enough as it is. Imagine what he'd be without me breathing down his neck.

COACH: Ok. Let's imagine that. What would it feel like to have complete permission to perform as you do, without any comparisons, to have absolute approval of your current results knowing that failures and successes don't define who you are? *(See Chapter 6, "On Your Perfect Moment.")*

Me: Oh my God, total relief. That would be amazing. But it feels untrue.

Critic: That's because it is untrue.

COACH: If you had such permission or approval would you cease your efforts? Would you lose your motivation or no longer have ambitions and plans or successes?

Me: I don't think so. Actually, I know that wouldn't happen. I would still have drive and goals and get things done. I'd make progress. I wouldn't be a slug.

Critic: You wouldn't be a slug but you wouldn't be a winner either.

COACH: What's a winner?

Critic: Someone who is always at the top of his game, focused, driven, disciplined.

COACH: Is that attainable?

Me: No, but I should be striving for it, shouldn't I?

COACH: Why?

Critic: Because he needs drive and focus and discipline. He needs goals and progress.

COACH: Doesn't he already have that?

Critic: Yeah, but not enough. And the need will never end.

COACH: So there'll always be a higher standard? Someplace further to go, higher to reach?

Me: Yeah, I suppose.

COACH: What is this constant comparison doing to you?

Critic: It's keeping him going. It's motivating. Without it he won't put forth the big effort.

Me: Actually, it kind of sucks. I either feel like I can't measure up to someone else or I get a fleeting ego boost compared to someone who I perceive as lesser. It's laughable because I don't know the situation of either person.

COACH: So this constant comparison sucks, it doesn't give you more drive or progress toward your goals yet you persist. Why?

Critic: I already told you it's because he needs to maintain high standards.

COACH: He has high standards.

Me: It seems like we're going around in circles and getting nowhere.

COACH: Exactly!

THE COACHING

"Daddy, you always say that." My daughter, Julia, was responding to my complaint that I hadn't accomplished as much at my desk as I had wanted to.

She continued somewhat mockingly, "You always say it wasn't good enough, or long enough, or productive enough."

Many years later my Aunt Penny, a wise and formidable woman, said, "My, what a shame. That must be very hard for you," when I confessed some guilt about watching a movie in the middle of a Sunday afternoon when there was so much else to do around the house.

She was referring not to the movie but to the fact that I wasn't able to enjoy it or its afterglow because I didn't have permission from the productivity police headquartered in my mind.

Both stories represent the unwinnable game of comparison to what's possible in any moment camouflaged as the pursuit of the highest standards in every moment.

Comparing one's present momentary effort to what's possible isn't like looking at a high bar to surmount but is more like looking at a horizon to touch by advancing toward it; something impossible to achieve.

We can never touch horizons because they exist only as points in space as one stands still. Comparing myself to what I know is possible in every situation is like striving to touch the horizon—as I advance, the standard moves further beyond reach.

This impossible quest is akin to the concept of the "hungry ghost" so poetically described in Buddhist cosmology. Renderings of these gruesome phantasms depict tiny necks and huge, insatiable bellies that represent desires that can never be fulfilled. Such is the appetite of the comparative critic.

The critic's constant comparisons and calls to do more, be more, reach farther, go faster, stay longer, be more productive, or always optimize are the sounds of the hungry ghost calling to be fed interminably.

"But what about high standards and stretch goals," we ask, "what about striving toward greater contributions or the pursuit of excellence?"

Those are worthy endeavors indeed. They should be part of every life journey. Along the way, however, we confuse the voice of the coach with that of the critic because they sometimes say the same things. *(See Chapter 9, "On Sucking It Up.")*

It is an inscrutable challenge to tease the two voices apart and there is only one way to do it—listen to the pitch. The distinction will soon be as obvious to you as an off key tenor is to a chorus director.

When our coach sings we feel left uplifted, inspired, and ready to do better and be more at the next opportunity. It may be difficult but we nod in agreement.

When the critic sings, squawks really, we feel stung by self-flagellation and diminished. We contract and we shake our heads in disgust at ourselves.

The voice of the coach is full of questions about the context of choices made and results attained. It is curious about reasons and situational dependencies. It wants to know what else is going on, what we can learn, what we can do differently next time.

The voice of the critic passes judgment uniformly. It always compares what was to what was possible, forever scolding for not arriving at the horizon. Our coach pulls us towards markers on this horizon. Our critic tells us we should be there already and compares us to those we think have arrived.

Because horizons move beyond reach in direct proportion to our advances, let our coach plant markers along the way. Then, when comparing critic squawks at us, we can point it rearward to demonstrate how far we've come.

THE NEXT STEP

My triathlon coach, Martha Grinnell, once told me, "When you compare yourself to others you give away your power. Don't race their race. Race your own."

1. Call to mind a frequent, deflating, comparison that you make in any context be it personal, professional, or relational. Write it here.

____

____

____

____

2. Give it a voice and read the comparison aloud. Immediately notice how this sound makes you feel. Describe it here. *(My first therapist asked me to do this, and an annoying chipmunk emerged. I found it grating and petty and therefore easy to dismiss.)*

____

____

____

____

3. Write what the voice of your coach-conscience could say in reply? *(In my case, replying to the chipmunk.)* If it's the same as the critic, try again.

____

____

____

____

4. Say it aloud and immediately notice how it sounds and makes you feel. Again, if it's the same as the critic, repeat step three. Describe it here.

____

____

____

____

An internal debate between your critic and your coach will likely emerge. Your critic is invested in winning. Your coach is committed to gains, no matter the size. To whom will you listen?

AFFIRMATION

Quietly repeat the following affirmation when you find yourself struggling with this chapter's dilemma or write your own using the DIY guide on page 175.

Today I have complete permission to be as I am.

I compare myself to no one because my journey is my own.

I feel good about my true self, and am excited to bring more of it into the world.

MY OWN AFFIRMATION

____

____

____

____

CHAPTER 6

ON YOUR PERFECT MOMENT

This moment, right now, whispers not a criticism but a choice.

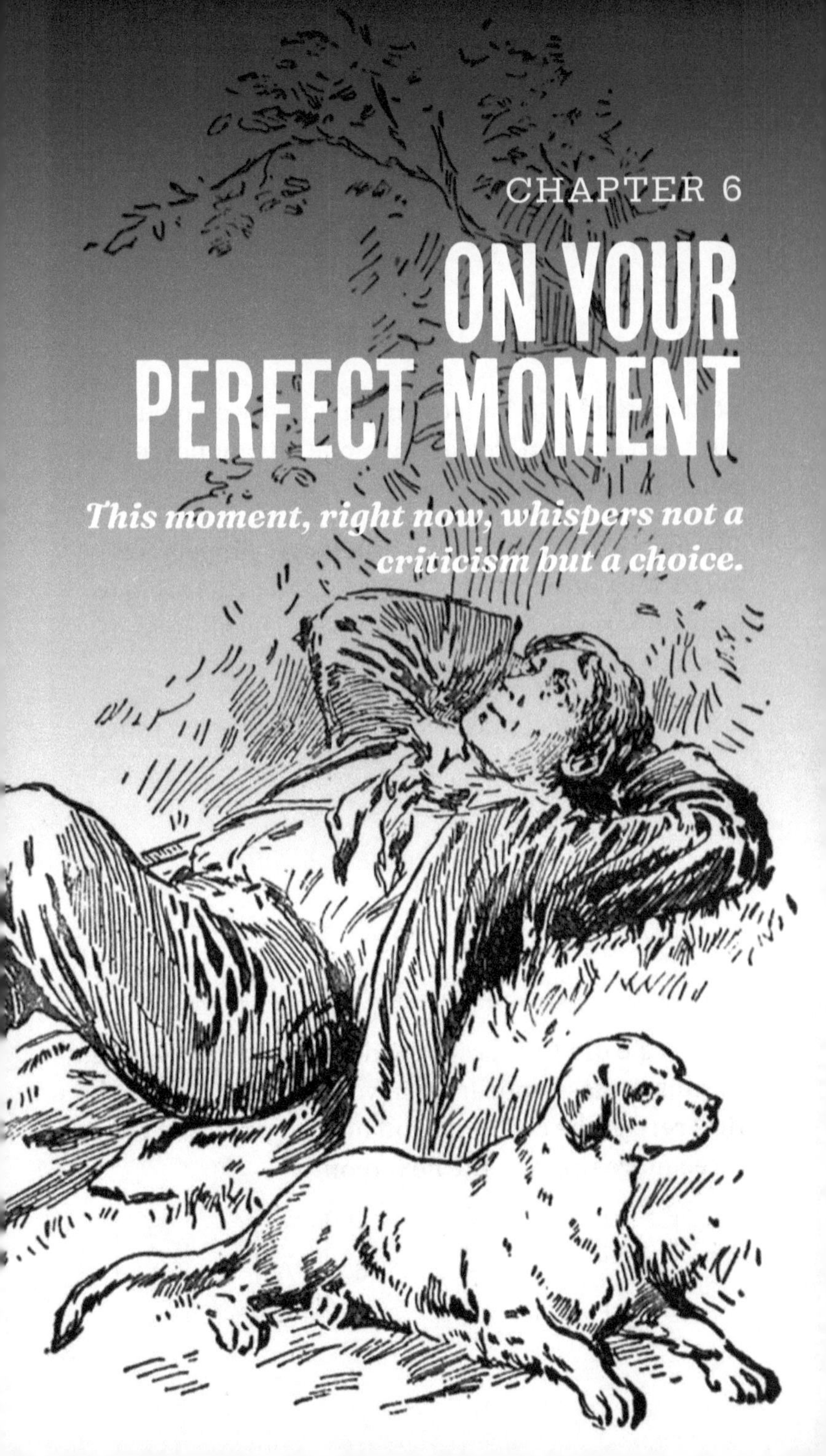

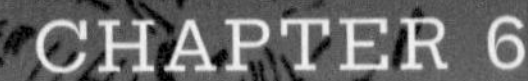

THE DILEMMA

I understand that I am the master of my own fate but I feel at the mercy of my mood, my money, or so much I can't control.

Prospective buyers are unresponsive, slippery, or jaded. My outreach feels fruitless and deals seem to drag on forever. I also feel hampered by all sorts of obstacles and pressure.

Often, I don't feel masterful; I feel miserable or meh.

How can I resolve this?

On a scale of 1 to 10, rate the degree to which you find this dilemma reappearing in your life. If it's more than five, reread the coaching and next steps of this chapter three more times in the next month.

| 1 | 2 | 3 | 4 | 5 | 6 | 7 | 8 | 9 | 10 |

THE TAKEAWAY

Read this chapter if your morale is low or you are in a place of difficulty, confusion, or pain.

This chapter will help you understand why you are exactly where you should be even if you dislike it.

You will gain a new perspective on your struggle and see how your destiny is revealed in your day.

It shows up in this dueling dialogue...

THE DUELING DIALOGUES

Me: Jeez, my belly is soft. I can barely button these pants. Thank God nobody can see me naked.

Critic: Yeah, that's embarrassing, fatty. You've been self-conscious about that forever.

COACH: Who would judge you naked?
What would they say?

Me: Everybody. You're fat. You're unattractive. You're unhealthy. You're undisciplined.

COACH: Ouch. What else are you?

Critic: Dumb question. Off topic. Whatever he says about his struggle and good intentions is irrelevant. We are talking about his body. He is overweight and undisciplined. It's unattractive and unhealthy.

Me: I'm ashamed to say it, but Critic is right. I'm basically resigned to it. It's really no biggie.

COACH: That's how you feel. What else are you?

Critic: Off topic. You're still ducking the truth. We already know what he is. He admitted it.

COACH: Shhhh, let him answer.

Me: I'm a man making my way in the world. My heart is in the right place. I'm trying. I have other areas where I actually perform well.

COACH: That's what you are doing, not what you are. What else are you?

Critic: Ugh! He's a carbon-based life form animated by electrical impulses vibrating at multitudinous frequencies. And he's fat. Don't let him duck his failings.

COACH: You're not entirely annoying, Critic. I like your first sentence. Now shush. Let him answer. What else are you?

Me: Lots of things. I'm a worker, a father, a friend, a citizen. I have hopes and desires in those domains, too.

COACH: Those are your roles and what you want. What else are you?

Me: I'm annoyed, what are you getting at?

COACH: Sorry. Clearing cobwebs is annoying. Do I have this right? You are a man quietly burdened with internalized judgment because your belly is soft because you've failed in your fitness plans despite your intentions, but with success in some domains, and aspirations in others, yes?

Me: Yes.

COACH: What if you were thin and ripped?

Me: Oh joy! I'd be free of my burden and all the judgments. Then I would ...

Critic: Still drive a crappy car, still be broke, still be fighting with your wife, and still be anxious.

COACH: Shush, Critic. You are like whack-a-mole. Let's let him answer. C'mon brother, what else are you?

Me: I don't know, man. I'm tired of your questions. I'm right here, right now, flowing along with eight billion other people on the planet living out their own moment-by-moment joys and struggles and aspirations in a great cosmic mystery.

COACH: Yes!

THE COACHING

You are right here, right now, living—barely or fully, happily or miserably. In this precise moment of time, this instant, your pants fit you exactly as they should because everything in your life, everything, has led you to this exact moment.

It is as it should be, and yet, it may feel so wrong. It's the same whether we are talking about your waistline, wallet, or worldview.

Conscious thought fills the entirety of your being. But it isn't you—it's thought. You feel ashamed or lazy or broke or lonely or like a fraud. And your critical, egoic mind will convince you on that particular day, in that particular circumstance, that it's true.

But on a different day at another moment it could all feel right. And it would be. In that instant of time, with your sales pipeline full and your waistline irrelevant, everything in your life, everything, led you to precisely that moment. You are full of joy and contentment.

You have a history but it vanished the instant you lived it. You have a future but it exists, no matter how well envisioned, only in your mind. Neither is right here, right now. Only you are. You and the choice you are about to make.

Eat the chips or the kale. Bemoan a circumstance or be strengthened by it. Make a cold call or dawdle at your desk. The now whispers not a criticism but a choice.

On one hand, your choice in any instant matters not one iota because you are nothing more than a faint ripple of energy in the cosmos. (AKA a carbon-based life form animated by electrical impulses vibrating at multitudinous frequencies.)

On the other hand, a single choice shapes outcomes and fills your conscious mind entirely. Those choices, strung together over a lifetime have made you—but it isn't really you. It's only partially you.

American Philosopher William Durant had it half right when he paraphrased Aristotle, "We are what we repeatedly do. Excellence, then, is not an act but a habit."

That perspective only captures the outer-world of your results made manifest by your choices, your soft (or ripped) belly as it were. Your inner-world, the unmanifest, doesn't say you are what you've done but simply, you are infinite possibility.

As Deepak Chopra's writings so elegantly remind us, it is a world of pure potential. It is therefore perfect, and you have already arrived.

I know this doesn't help when you are below quota, gravely ill, or feeling pudgy. But it's true nevertheless. All you have is now and you are in it. The past is exactly that. The future is a figment.

In this same instant you are both the product of choice and the possibility in choice. You are full of infinite possibility and this is why your pants fit you exactly as they should.

THE NEXT STEP

1. First, remember that all humans carry
    pain and doubt and struggle, even those
    whom you most admire.

2. Complete this short exercise if you are feeling
    anxious or sad for any reason. It will create
    some mental space to respond from a place of
    power instead of pain.

    A. Find a quiet, solitary place preferably with
        some beauty visible.

    B. Sit comfortably. Put a soft smile on your face
        and take three deep, long, slow breaths as you
        sink into your seat.

    C. Relax your face and the rest of your body
        while you allow all your pressing worries,
        ruminations, or impulses to chatter in your
        mind's ear. The depth or the nature of the
        chatter doesn't matter—it's yours.

    D. Notice the chatter but don't evaluate it. You will
        evaluate it, but notice your evaluating. Don't
        follow a particular train of thought but allow
        it to pass in and out of your focus like scrolling

words on an electronic sign or like leaves floating down a creek. Just keep watching it come and go. Do this for two minutes.

E. Continue watching the thoughts and then turn your attention to where in your body you feel a particular worry. Place your hand there and whisper to yourself as if you were soothing a scared seven-year-old.

F. What would you say? Write the kindest, most loving thing you can think of here. Begin the sentence with, *"I know that you feel...*

____

____

____

____

3. If what you wrote to yourself feels inauthentic or thin, rewrite it until it feels authentic and loving.

4. Say it aloud, slowly. Breathe it in.

AFFIRMATION

Quietly repeat the following affirmation when you find yourself struggling with this chapter's dilemma or write your own using the DIY guide on page 175.

I am an infinite choice maker therefore infinite possibilities are mine.

MY OWN AFFIRMATION

____

____

____

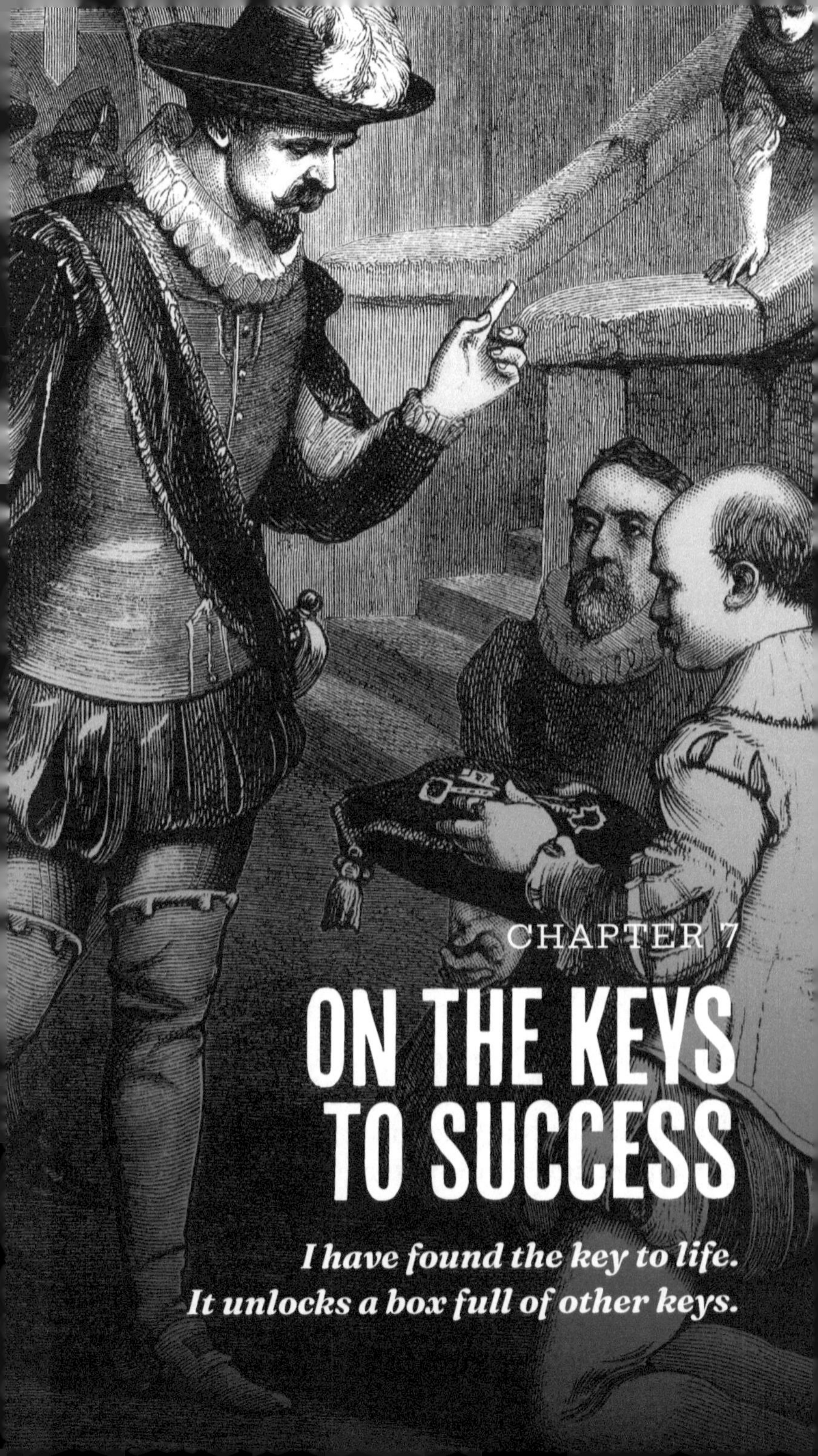

CHAPTER 7

ON THE KEYS TO SUCCESS

I have found the key to life.
It unlocks a box full of other keys.

THE DILEMMA

There is such an endless stream of resources on how to optimize every element of my life that I don't know where to begin, whom to trust, or how to prioritize what's actually best for me.

I find myself constantly drawn to the latest and greatest ways to improve my health, my relationships, my fitness, my mindset, my business, my skills, and my habits.

This fitful dabbling in tips and tricks doesn't help me feel I'm getting better but rather like I'm missing out on the best ways to improve my journey or speed things along.

On a scale of 1 to 10, rate the degree to which you find this dilemma reappearing in your life. If it's more than five, reread the coaching and next steps of this chapter three more times in the next month.

| 1 | 2 | 3 | 4 | 5 | 6 | 7 | 8 | 9 | 10 |

THE TAKEAWAY

Read this chapter if you are frequently drawn to self-help or business and personal- improvement resources, or you often look for hacks to optimize your life—everything from sales production to your wellness, your work, or your wealth.

This chapter will relieve you of the nagging sense that you may be missing the secrets to improved performance or some best practice to shortcut the long journey towards mastery of any aspect of your life.

You will discover the keys to excellence in all domains can be distilled into just five powerful practices drawn from the wisdom of the ages.

It shows up in this dueling dialogue...

THE DUELING DIALOGUE

Critic: You idiot. You wasted $600.

Me: I know, I know, I was sure it would be different this time.

Critic: You said that last time, and the time before that. Always the same.

Me: True, but dammit this wasn't a free webinar, it was $600 so I'm committed to completing the entire program. I'm even keeping the course link in my inbox so that it stays top of mind.

Critic: Dude, the link has been in your inbox for five months and you still haven't followed through! You do stuff like this all the time. *(See Chapter 3, "On Failed Intentions.")*

Me: Dammit, I know. But it really is something I want to do. It's an important topic and I find it fascinating.

COACH: What does he mean by "You do stuff like this all the time?"

Me: I often click on a course link, subscribe to a program, join a webinar, or buy a book with the promise of some transformation. I admit, I'm a junkie for always trying to find better ways.

COACH: A better way to what?

Me: Hell, to a bunch of things: more energy, higher productivity, improved mindset, increased fitness, new skills, better memory, you name it.

COACH: I hear you, that pool is bottomless and enticing. I love swimming there, too. But what drew you to the course?

Me: Oh crap, I don't even remember. I'm sure it was an email from some list or resource I'm subscribed to or it was a referral link from an expert or source I respect.

Critic: Sucker. So gullible and distractible. He wasn't even thinking about this topic before. He's just got shiny object syndrome. *(See Chapter 8, "On Finding Flow Amidst Your ADHD.")*

COACH: I like shiny objects, too. But I'm asking him, what were you looking for?

Me: Nothing in particular. The title just struck me and the marketing was great and the free webinar leading to the pitch was compelling so I bought it.

Critic: He got sucked in like he always does, by the promise of some silver bullet, secret sauce, or big breakthrough in his life.

COACH: What's wrong with that?

Critic: He halfway or never follows through. Plus, he doesn't remember a damn thing.

COACH: Nope. That's being human. What's the problem with looking for answers or better ways of being and doing and living?

Me: Well, I suppose the search is endless or I end up expectantly tugging on a thousand different strands.

COACH: You are getting close. It's not the searching that's flawed, nor even the tugging on strands. What are you grasping at?

Critic: He wants things to be easier.

COACH: That's fair, don't we all. C'mon brother, you're almost there.

Me: Oh, I suppose it comes down to some form of reassurance or confidence that I'm on the right track. I want guidance about the best way to get through life.

COACH: Yes! We are all trying to find the way to our best life. But your search has you grasping at random keys hoping you find the right one instead of holding a key ring to select carefully.

Me/Critic: Huh?

COACH: Picture the loaded keyrings of a janitor or a maintenance foreman. When he wants to unlock any door in his massive building, what does he do?

Me: He picks a key from his ring.

COACH: Exactly. In this case, there are only five. Let's choose one together.

THE COACHING

In my hunger for improvement in nearly every element of my life I can be seduced by the pursuit of the best performance hacks or keys to success—those small but elusive shifts that yield a dramatic impact on my results, experience, or behavior.

Even when I find a sensible hack and can sustain it, say waking up early, amidst the countless success tips that exist in all of life's domains, I am soon on the quest for another hack.

After decades of swinging from anxiety, avoidance, or frenzy in the morning, I finally found great success with early rising, holding precious that first 90 minutes of my day. The time when, to hear Thoreau describe it, all poets and heroes emit their music, all intelligences awaken, and the soul of man is reinvigorated.

I developed this hard-won habit to greet the dawn with an unwitting assist from other people. It was at early-morning track workouts and the pool where I agreed to meet training partners during my first year of racing triathlons that broke the pre-dawn inertia.

The self-imposed peer pressure and the limited free time I had as a busy father, homemaker, caregiver, and business owner forced me into a new routine. And thus a hack became a habit.

Despite this success, I can still feel unsatisfied and bounce from seeking a silver bullet to a secret sauce, flitting in multiple directions, sometimes taking detours that ultimately lead nowhere. *(See Chapter 5, "On Not Being Good Enough.")*

Consequently, I no longer search the landscape for performance hacks but instead scan my behaviors for the presence of five master keys that always unlock improved performance.

What are the keys to high performance, to greater joy and success in our careers, our relationships, and our wellness?

We see them everywhere. If we were lucky, the influential adults in our lives, be they caregivers, teachers, mentors, or ministers, taught them to us. We feel them jingling in our pockets with great regularity. But, like keys in one's pocket, we grow oblivious to their presence.

There is no single key to a life well lived—there are five master keys.

I have studied wisdom literature, everything from the Bible to the Bhagavad Gita, from the Stoics of Ancient

Greece to modern day masters like the Dalai Lama and Deepak Chopra.

I read everything I could find and took notes, made lists, compared, contrasted, and noticed that the same five master keys emerged.

We can call them keys, success habits, rules, principals, or fundamentals. It doesn't matter what term we use, we can distill their essence to the same five, dichotomous elements.

These five elements are dichotomous because they simultaneously occupy our private, inner-world of belief, thought, and feeling, and our public, outer-world of action and results.

The five master keys to life are:

1. **Self-awareness.** This is the domain of quietude and reflection. Beneath the clutter of our unconscious inner dialogue, we uncover our deepest thoughts and feelings, which not only enable conscious choice making but also help us recognize our interconnectedness with other beings and our oneness with the universe.

   Here vanity turns to humility, selfishness to selflessness, and reactivity to restraint.

Curiosity, flexibility, and receptivity are the watch words as we repeatedly answer the single deepest question we can ask about ourselves: why?

"Why am I so impatient with my wife? Why do I get so angry at political partisans? Why am I so judgmental or critical or shy or brash? Why am I feeling anxious, afraid, apathetic, or angry?"

Why?

The only way to answer such questions is to quietly look inward. Here we will find the source of our strength, volition, and response to all stimuli. For many people, this is where God is found.

I freely admit to profound doubt about my choice to be a solopreneur sales coach early in my career. For years I struggled with financial anxiety, I was short-fused and scattered yet still felt compelled to stay the course.

It was only through repeated introspection, a byproduct of psychotherapy, that I was able to ground myself in the value I deliver and the skills I could sharpen. Thus grounded, I knew I would be ok on a path that takes time.

I look back on the journey grateful for the anxiety, doubt, and struggle, and the gifts they helped me develop, happy to have arrived at a place where I enjoy a strong reputation and successful business.

☘ If you want to hack self-awareness, develop a mindfulness practice such as journaling or meditation. Spend time in deep reflection or psychotherapy or both. A strong assist can come from reading uplifting spiritual writings. *(See Chapter 6, "On Your Perfect Moment.")*

2. **Goal pursuit.** Hunt and forage or die. Even if it's only towards our next meal, we must advance. If pure survival is at one end of the spectrum, the other end contains missions and visions, a purpose, or a raison d'être.

   Be it a grand ambition or a small step, we must have ends in mind. This doesn't mean we aren't also rooted in the present moment, which is the most fertile ground for choice making.

   Sometimes the best choice is to sit and wonder. But always the hunt must resume.

   Looking back, I can see clear demarcations in the process of all my most ambitious undertakings. This book, for example, came to fruition only when, after many years of languishing and sputtering, I decided, dammit, it had to get done.

   That transition from nice idea to firm resolve unleashed all manner of forces and proved Goethe's insight to be true, "That the moment one definitely commits oneself, then Providence moves, too."

The pursuit, be it for a sale, a trophy, health, or love, is part of our animating force. This is the domain of clear intention and fierce desire but without attachment to outcome because, ultimately, we have no control over outcome. *(See Chapter 2, "On Accountability.")*

- If you want to hack goal attainment stretch for something big and far and meaningful that inspires you. (Along the way, you'll want to quit, which is why you need the fifth key, practice.)

3. **Self-Care.** Although we are metaphysical beings, we inhabit mortal bodies that need tending. Good nutrition, fitness, sleep, play, and strong relationships occupy this domain.

   We must attend to our heart and mind as much as we do our soul, which brings us full circle back to self-awareness. In this case, awareness of what we read, watch, study, and the company we keep.

   We become what we repeatedly consume—be it grease, gossip, or greatness. And because we are the vessel through which the designs of the universe are made manifest, we must care for the self at every level.

We must observe the routines that become our patterns that become the habits that serve our highest self or our lowest.

I spent many years of my life saying I'm not a morning person, until I became one. That single habit, rising early, paved the way for sundry other self-care habits to bloom: reading, writing, meditation, and exercise. (Not checking email!)

Author Charles Duhigg describes this phenomenon, one healthy habit unleashing others, as a keystone habit. That first habitual behavior thus becomes a platform from which others launch.

- If you want to hack self-care, wake up 45 minutes earlier than normal and go for a brisk walk outside.

  (Oh, and to accomplish this, you may want to go to bed earlier and get a good night's sleep. To do this, you might need to shut down your screens earlier, and avoid sugar, caffeine, or calories too late in the day. And if you are going to practice sleep hygiene you should probably start planning meals, which means you should … Too much? Yeah, probably. How about you just try waking up early tomorrow and see what happens? Try again and again and again. It will get easier. You will reap rewards.)

4. **Service.** This is the domain of community and caring, and dare I say, love. Service means giving, which surprisingly, includes empathy and forgiveness.

    When we are wronged by another person, giving is the last thing on our mind but is the first step in repair: give up our venom and give in to understanding, that core element of empathy and a prerequisite to forgiveness. *(See Chapter 10, "On Gratitude and Forgiveness.")*

    Service means we offer our resources of time, energy, and money, and as an unintended consequence they come back to us in unpredictable ways. This circularity is why we must also gratefully receive while we generously give.

    Our charitable words and deeds, be they quiet prayers or heroic gestures toward people and causes, always cycle. Call it karma, reciprocity, or reaping what we sow; what goes around comes around.

    Service also feels good. Neuroscientific studies confirm that giving uncorks a flood of neurotransmitters such as serotonin and dopamine that counteract stress hormones and stimulate feelings of wellness and peace.

    The payoff isn't just karmic, it's chemical.

Service can also be inconvenient and time consuming. It will cost us money, effort, and attention. But dang it, sometimes we just have to sign up to volunteer for that committee role because it is our turn, or contribute to the fundraiser because our neighbor asked.

Gratitude and compassion live here because we recognize our blessings even in the midst of our struggles or suffering. We give to and care for others even though we may still have unmet wants and needs.

Take, for example, your desire to have calls and emails returned, for prospects to give you a listen, for courtesy. Because I want that in my life, I make an effort to listen to anyone going door to door. With every telemarketing call, I try to be courteous and respectful because that's what I want, knowing as I do what it's like to be easily dismissed or ignored.

⚡ If you want to hack service, give at three levels:

I. Replace your critical judgment of anyone with a blessing. Forgive someone who has wronged you.

II. Become a monthly sustaining giver in any amount to any charitable cause that speaks to you.

III. Tip well, look panhandlers in the eye even if
you don't give money, and volunteer.

5. **Practice.** You will repeat everything until you
die. Your lessons and insights, and your efforts
and results, all cycle. So too with blind spots
and inaction. This means we have countless
opportunities to grow because the cycle never ends.

In the psycho-spiritual sense, practice is
the recurring process of self-examination,
particularly our triggers and negative patterns. It
is reconnection by countless means to the deepest
reservoirs of our humanity.

Prayers, yoga, meditation, and introspection
only work their magic when they are
repeated again and again.

In the behavioral sense, practice is the domain
of feedback, standards, and metrics. Here skills
sharpen, effort pays off, and reboots are welcome.

Study, exertion, rehearsal, and review
only work their magic when they are
repeated again and again.

Thus, it is only through practice that we learn to act
greater than we feel anytime the going gets tough.
We will feel apathy and anxiety, we will feel like
a once gleaming goal is no longer that important.
We'll want to quit, we'll rationalize, and minimize.

It takes practice to act greater than those feelings. *(See Chapter 3, "On Failed Intentions.")*

Because what we focus on grows and what we neglect withers, repetition always wins the day. Did I say practice never ends?

>  If you want to hack practice be both forgiving and disciplined with yourself as you keep progress not perfection in your sights. Failures, frustrations, and false starts litter the entire journey. That's why it's practice—even on game day. *(See Chapter 8, "On Finding Flow Amidst Your ADD.")*

We can demoralize and paralyze ourselves with inaction—seeking hacks for any one of these five master keys—because each one is so multifaceted.

The same is true if we ponder the multilayered complexity of sales success:

> *"Holy cow! Here are ten books on making cold calls, and here are twenty others on closing the sale. Oh, and look over there, one hundred titles on time management."*

Instead of constantly scanning for the right or best hack in any element of your life, say selling, we are better served by digging narrow and deep into a single skill, say follow up discipline, and then practice, practice, practice.

To dabble broad and shallow is fine as an experimental exercise but it gives us no purchase.

If self-care is the goal, better to buy a single cookbook about preparing delicious and nutritious meals and then doing so five nights a week, week after week. There, that's the hack—buy and use the cookbook.

But be warned. Until they are habitual, your hacks will be fleeting on any path to mastery.

However, mastery itself is misleading because it implies that you've arrived. There is no arriving at self-care mastery simply because the process never ends—so too with self-awareness, goal pursuit, service, and practice.

Each of these five master keys unlocks the door to a complicated subject, yet walking into the room is ultimately quite simple. Focus with integrity on the simple, and the complex will take care of itself. *(See Chapter 2, "On Accountability.")*

THE NEXT STEP

— PART ONE —

1. Briefly review the five master keys described in this chapter and select the one that presently feels the most neglected. Write it here:

   ____

2. Take a moment to reflect on the master key you wrote above, and think of two simple actions you could take in the next 36 hours to jigger a lock. Write them here:

   ____

   ____

   ____

3. If you need to, replace your "I should or I could" language with "I will" and then pick one of the two actions above. Refine it here if need be and do it now. If you can't do it now, schedule a time to do it in the next 12 hours.

   ____

   ____

4. Repeat this process once more in the next week. Do this for two more weeks and you'll have a full month of weekly practice.

— PART TWO —

1. Next, anytime you hear yourself negatively judging someone else, complete the sentence you silently heard yourself utter with the words "Just like me."

    ⚕ *For example: "That person is such a jerk, just like me." (If that doesn't ring true for you, ask yourself how or why that person is a jerk, then try again. For example, "That person is such a jerk because he's so opinionated, just like me."*

    If you are aware of recurring negative judgements you carry about someone, say a political figure, try the exercise right now. Write the complete sentence here:

    ____

    ____

    ____

    If you don't think that whomever you judge is *just like you*, dig two or three layers beneath your protective surface and you will find elements of yourself.

AFFIRMATION

Quietly repeat the following affirmation when you find yourself struggling with this chapter's dilemma or write your own using the DIY guide on page 175.

I deepen my self-understanding and love for who I am so I can take meaningful action.

MY OWN AFFIRMATION

____

____

____

____

CHAPTER 8

ON FINDING FLOW AMIDST YOUR ADHD/ADD

I have come far, oh great guru.
Pray tell me the secret to...
HEY LOOK, a squirrel!

THE DILEMMA

I frequently struggle to stay on task and, as a result, have so many open loops that things take me a long time to complete, if I complete them at all.

I start and stop frequently, and get distracted or bored so easily that it's often challenging for me to find a rhythm or flow.

In the end, I feel frustrated by my slow pace, overwhelmed by loose ends, and resigned to my scattered brain.

How can I resolve this?

On a scale of 1 to 10, rate the degree to which you find this dilemma reappearing in your life. If it's more than five, reread the coaching and next steps of this chapter three more times in the next month.

| 1 | 2 | 3 | 4 | 5 | 6 | 7 | 8 | 9 | 10 |

THE TAKEAWAY

Read this chapter if you identify with Attention Deficit Disorder with or without hyperactivity (ADHD/ADD*). You may frequently joke that you have it or you may have received a clinical diagnosis confirming it. In either case, you recognize your halting effectiveness.

This chapter dispels the notion that ADD is a disorder to overcome and flips it on its head as an asset to be leveraged called DDA (Dynamically Directed Attention).

You will understand how ADD can impede the four components of flow, and how to transform those impediments into accelerants so that you can access flow states more easily and often.

It shows up in this dueling dialogue...

---

* Technically speaking, ADD is not a standalone diagnosis but rather a component of the more clinically accurate abbreviation, ADHD (Attention Deficit Hyperactivity Disorder) as described in *The Diagnostic and Statistical Manual of Mental Disorders, Fifth Edition.*

THE DUELING DIALOGUE

Critic: Yo, check out this other video clip. It's even more hilarious.

Me: Last one, man, then I need to concentrate on this project.

Critic: Good luck. You've been saying that all morning.

Me: I know but you keep interrupting me. I'm gonna get a big chunk of it done now.

Critic: What about those two things on your desk that still need attention?

Me: Oh, shoot, you're right. I can bang out one of them right now. It should be quick.

COACH: I thought you were going to buckle down on your project right now.

Me: I will, but first I need to finish up this other task. It won't take that long and it's been hanging over my head for a while.

COACH: When is it due?

Me: There's no hard deadline but, hold on a sec, I need a snack.

Critic: What are you doing, man, sit back down.

Me: Nah, I'm getting antsy. Gotta move.

Critic: Damn, dude, just finish what you're doing. There's not that much left anyway.

Me: Yeah, I hear ya. But I can't concentrate on it anymore. I'll come back to it in a bit.

Critic: You say that all the time, and then something else pops up to distract you.

Me: Maybe, but most of the time I find my way back.

COACH: How do you keep things from slipping through the cracks?

Critic: He doesn't.

Me: Mostly I remember, or I set an alarm or a timer, or I scribble notes to myself.

COACH: That sounds smart.

Critic: Ha! He's got little notes all over the place, and bells constantly ringing.

COACH: So what?

Critic: It's friggin' noisy, plus it's super inefficient and stuff slips through the cracks.

Me: I know, I know, but what you need to understand is, hang on a sec, I need to grab this call.

Critic: Classic.

COACH: I don't mind waiting.

Me: Ok, all set. Just gimme a minute to send this email.

Critic: That figures.

COACH: I'll wait. Can the email?

Me: Yeah, sure, but I just now agreed to send a document. It'll only take a sec.

COACH: I'll wait.

Critic: Grrrrr!

Me: Damn! This document formatting is all whacky. I can't send it like this. Hang on.

Critic: What'd I tell ya?

Me: Ok, all set. Thanks for waiting. Where were we?

Critic: You were jumping around.

COACH: We were talking about inefficiency and switching from task to task.

Me: Oh yeah, efficiency. I've heard it a thousand times, the shortest distance between two points is a straight line.

Critic: Exactly! And your roads to completion look like EKGs.

COACH: Are you saying he takes a windy, slow road?

Critic: Yep. It's super inefficient. And he drops all kinds of stuff along the way.

COACH: Do you always arrive with what you need, and are you able to retrieve what you left behind?

Me: Yeah, pretty much.

Critic: Except for all those intentions that are dead from neglect.

COACH: Dead or dormant?

Me: What's the difference?

COACH: Something dormant can reawaken.

Critic: Fits and starts, man.

COACH: But he gets there.

Critic: After so many detours.

COACH: Why do you take the detours?

Me: Because I see something I want to explore, I remember something I left behind, I lose focus, I get bored.

COACH: How long has that been the case?

Me: Since I was a kid.

COACH: Why do you keep fighting it?

Me: Because I know the straight line is more efficient.

COACH: But you're going through the mountains and the valleys.

Critic: He needs a plane.

COACH: But he's driving a car.

THE COACHING

I can recall many times I was in the zone or in the groove. These were states of high performance. I wasn't aware of time because I was completely immersed in the moment doing something both challenging and gratifying. It was an optimal experience of total presence without another care in the world.

You have been there too, I'm sure of it.

Perhaps you spent all morning building a sand castle, a stone wall, or a carpentry project. Maybe you were sculpting, or gardening, or playing a sonata. Maybe you were surfing, or dancing, or ripping downhill on skis or a mountain bike. You could have been writing, or coding, or trail running.

When you recall peak experiences you do so with deep satisfaction and perhaps some yearning because they felt so great. It is during such times that we experience what researchers call a flow state, a term coined by Hungarian-born psychologist, Mihaly Csikszentmihalyi.

If I shift my memory to the other end of the spectrum, that is, not in flow, I can easily recall experiences of inattention, impulsivity, forgetfulness, or failure to follow through.

Often, I am unable to maintain my focus or am so hyperfocused that I miss other pressing tasks. I can feel lost or frustrated or like a failure compared to everyone else who seems to complete tasks in a timely way with far less effort. *(See Chapter 5, "On Not Being Good Enough.")*

If you struggle as I do with ADD, it won't be hard for you to summon such memories, either. But imagine experiencing a flow state or approaching a flow state more often, longer, and across a wider range of pursuits.

A flow state is a beautiful thing but it needn't be limited to a narrow band of activities. Nor is it reserved for peak performers or people who don't struggle with ADD. We can bring all of the elements of flow to our more quotidian pursuits.

The clinical definition of a flow state derived by Hungarian-American psychologist, Mihaly Csikszentmihalyi, the pioneering researcher considered the father of flow, is a mouthful:

> "A sense that one's skills are adequate to cope with the challenges at hand in a goal directed, rule-bound action system that provides clear clues as to

how one is performing. Concentration is so intense that there is no attention left over to think about anything irrelevant or to worry about problems. Self-consciousness disappears, and the sense of time becomes distorted. An activity that produces such experiences is so gratifying that people are willing to do it for its own sake, with little concern for what they will get out of it, even when it is difficult or dangerous."

Phew! Here it is again in slow motion.

If we break down that super-sized definition into four bite-size chunks, flow requires us to have:

1. **Clear goals** and immediate feedback. (In other words, your objective is clear and you have instantaneous ways to stay on target.)

2. **Equilibrium** between the level of challenge and personal skill. (In other words, your skill to challenge ratio is balanced. Too much skill + not enough challenge = bored. Too much challenge + not enough skill = anxious.)

3. **Focused concentration.** (In other words, the quality of your attention in a given moment is high.)

4. **Loss of self-consciousness** and a distortion of time. (In other words, you don't give a damn what people think or say because you are lost in time.)

Wow, wouldn't it be great to live there more often! My problem is that so much of my experience of self seems to contradict each component of flow.

1. Clear goals and immediate feedback? Nope. The objects of my attention are many, I can scarcely hold them, and my feedback loops are often critical.

2. Balanced skill to challenge ratio? Nope. I can swing between overly ambitious agreements with high hopes, to complete avoidance or repetition of what's easy and familiar.

3. Intense concentration? Nope. I'm easily distracted, often lack focus, and struggle to listen well or remember details.

4. Unselfconscious and unhurried? Nope. I feel frustrated and impatient by how long things take me. And I am overly invested in being liked.

Damn! That experience is the opposite of a flow state. But it needn't be.

The reason we ADDers have such a hard time finding flow is because we fight against our own biochemistry. If we embrace who we are without capitulation then we wouldn't have to exert such tremendous effort at such a high cost to be satisfied with our results. We would find flow states more often.

On good days my ADD isn't a disorder at all but an asset I've turned on its head to become what I call DDA (Dynamically Directed Attention). Using the four components of a flow state in reverse order, here's how I've turned ADD upside down so that it serves me instead of saddles me.

4. I become conscious of my unconscious by tuning into my mental chatter. I listen to my self-talk. I remind myself that I am not the negative story my mind makes up but rather an infinite choice maker right where I am supposed to be. I am what I am, where I am, why I am. Then I ask, what's next?

3. If deciding what's next and holding focus on a particular task is too hard in a particular moment, I allow my impulsive mind to grab a new object of attention. Sometimes I don't allow so much as unwittingly succumb. I simply bring a notepad and a timer along for the ride so I can create the breadcrumb trail leading back to my accountabilities. *(See Chapter 2, "On Accountability.")*

2. Whether I get back on target in ten seconds or ten days or never, I get to choose anew how to balance my attention. The breadcrumb trail leading back to my accountabilities contains my lists, notes, micro-

deadlines, and a countdown clock. I also give my physical body what it needs in terms of hydration, nutrition, and exercise.

1. Along the entire path I listen for the forgiving whisper instead of the critical hiss to provide accurate, timely feedback. *(See Chapter 9, "On Sucking It Up.")* One steers me back on course toward chosen goals. The other buffets me against the rocks of regret and recrimination. The coach looks ahead. The critic looks arear.

When I successfully tie all of those components together ADD becomes DDA and I have the best chance to find flow.

One of my favorite lessons in white-water guiding is "Go with the flow." This is not *hakuna matata*, take it easy man, just chill out and enjoy the ride kind of guidance. Certainly it could be, but I'm talking about not fighting the strength of a river current that forces me to spin off my desired line after clipping a rock or missing an eddy that I was trying to catch. Going with the flow in those circumstances means work with the river, not against it.

In my early years as a river guide, I'd strain to keep my boat straight. I'd strain to recover from an unintentional spin. I'd strain to do all the steering instead of commanding my crew of six to do some work.

Sometimes there is no choice but draw or pry hard
to stay on course but more often it's easier and just
as effective to let the river have its way, with nothing
more than a bit of steering from me to go with the flow.

THE NEXT STEP

1. Call to mind the most efficient, productive person you know. See them on a plane flying straight overhead. Smile at the distance they cover. Don't scowl that you aren't aboard. Write their name here:

    ____

2. Now see yourself packing the trunk of your car for a road trip to the same place. Smile knowing you will get there too, provided you pack the four essentials needed for every trip.

    Quietly conduct a yes/no inventory by asking yourself, "Do I have ..."

    A. A picture of my destination. (That is to say, do I have a clear goal in mind? Did I specify an outcome or purpose for my trip? What's my level of commitment to arriving at this goal in the next hour or next month?)

    YES   NO

B. A multi-tool to account for deadlines, regardless of their distance. (That is to say, am I willing to use a stopwatch, a timer, and a calendar at least as much as I use food and water?)

YES   NO

C. A roadside assistance plan. (That is to say, can I access other people to help me get unstuck, provide directions, or make repairs? Do I know how to find and use support?)

YES   NO

D. Ass glue, used sparingly. (That is to say, can I stick my ass to the seat and stay longer, go farther, or push beyond my first impulse to get up, switch tasks, or quit?

YES   NO

3. With your goal, tools, and support in hand, hit the road. But double your estimate of how long a trip takes. This will reduce your frustration with the inevitable detours.

4. Enjoy the scenery and the pace. You are on a road trip after all.

AFFIRMATION

Quietly repeat the following affirmation when you find yourself struggling with this chapter's dilemma or write your own using the DIY guide on page 175.

I maintain my natural rhythm and flow, gently guiding myself where I need to be.

MY OWN AFFIRMATION

____

____

____

____

CHAPTER 9

ON SUCKING IT UP

THE DILEMMA

I often scold myself for not being stronger when times are tough, the work is heavy or I feel anxious or like quitting.

As a consequence, I feel some shame for not having more strength, discipline, or endurance when I need it or think I should have it.

My attempts at self-understanding or forgiveness feel more like excuses and rationalizations than they do self-motivating.

How can I find a more consistent way to toughen up without feeling lame about myself when I don't?

On a scale of 1 to 10, rate the degree to which you find this dilemma reappearing in your life. If it's more than five, reread the coaching and next steps of this chapter three more times in the next month.

| 1 | 2 | 3 | 4 | 5 | 6 | 7 | 8 | 9 | 10 |

THE TAKEAWAY

Read this chapter if during times of inaction, avoidance, or anxiety you frequently berate, scold, or otherwise criticize yourself for not having more grit.

This chapter exposes the trap set by barking at yourself as the default means to motivation because it quickly morphs into criticism. You will understand how this drains your inner strength and how unsustainable it is as a source of fuel.

More importantly, you will learn to find the elusive balance point between barking and urging, between a press on the shoulder and a kick in the ass.

It shows up in this dueling dialogue...

THE DUELING DIALOGUE

Me: Man, I'm spent. I need a break.

Critic: Suck it up, dude. Everyone else manages just fine.

Me: Yeah, but I'm getting nowhere with my prospecting recently.

Critic: That's for sure!

Me: It's demoralizing. I need to do something else.

Critic: Quit sniveling. It's what you signed up for.

Me: I know, I know. It's just that ...

COACH: He signed up to be demoralized?

Critic: It's part of the territory.

COACH: Being demoralized? How?

Critic: Selling is his job! He should quit whining about how tough it is and get cranking.

COACH: I often see him cranking.

Critic: Not now. He's stopping.

COACH: Why?

Critic: Who cares, he's quitting.

COACH: Are you quitting?

Me: Man, I sure feel like it. I'm even doubting whether this job is sustainable.

Critic: See, I told you. Wuss.

COACH: He said feels like quitting, not actually quitting—two different things, man. Let him answer, why are you stopping, brother?

Me: As I said, I'm spent, just not feeling it these days, today especially. Sales aren't happening, I'm not reaching prospects, they don't respond to messages, and they're evasive or jaded. Ugh, I need a reset.

Critic: Quit complaining. You don't need a reset, dude, you need to double down on effort.

Me: I hear ya, it's just that ...

COACH: Where? Where should he double down on effort?

Critic: What do you mean where? Hell, everywhere! He ain't selling!

COACH: Focus everywhere can't be done—it's contradictory. Answer my question, Critic, where should he double down on effort?

Critic: F'n figure it out.

COACH: I think he's trying to. It's called a reset—take a little space, reassess, revitalize.

Critic: Bull crap. He's feeling weak and he's stopping when he should be sucking it up and cranking.

Me: He's right, I just need to suck it up.

COACH: How is sucking it up gonna help?

Me: It'll get me through the day.

COACH: Brother, I want to get you through the year. Hell, the decade!

Critic: He'll never last that long at this rate.

COACH: True that. Sucking it up day after day is no long term plan; I mean if you want some joy in your work.

Me: I'm certainly not feeling that today.

Critic: Stop being so weak.

COACH: Ignore him, brother; feeling weak isn't being weak.

Critic: Weak pipeline, weak sales, weak salesman. He's complaining when he should be doubling down on effort.

COACH: Critic is saying you are a weak salesman because you have weak sales because you have a weak pipeline. Repeat what he said but substitute the word strong. Where do you end up?

Me: Strong pipeline.

COACH: What makes a strong pipeline?

Me: Strong prospecting.

COACH: Exactly! Prospecting. Let's talk about that.

Me: Uuuugh, really?

COACH: No, not now. Let's go exercise for an hour. We'll make a new prospecting plan when we get back.

THE COACHING

You have to be able to suck it up and do what needs doing despite any resistance you feel. You must be able to drive on, to persevere, to not complain, and git 'er done.

Many of us call this soldiering on, an attribute extolled by the 3rd century Stoics as courage. Researchers sometimes call it grit, a term popularized by American academic and author Angela Duckworth in her seminal book, *Grit:The Power of Passion and Perseverance.*

The term we apply to ourselves doesn't matter. I use them all interchangeably for myself because ultimately each of us needs to summon some form of inner strength during countless moments of choice and challenge.

We are so often weak. We cave in. We quit. We complain. We don't follow through. And often, our excuses follow immediately behind.

But imagine an inner drill sergeant forcing us forward. He would have no patience nor tolerate a single rationalization or justification for our failures of will.

He would scream at us to get up and get going without an iota of concern for our feelings.

At so many levels, we need an inner drill sergeant who impels us to act greater than we may feel in any moment of choice:

- Make the cold calls when our sales pipeline is weak

- Get up earlier when we want to sleep later

- Stay longer when we want to leave sooner

- Hold our tongue when we want to lash out or complain

- Run the extra mile, do the extra rep, endure the heat, the cold, the wait

But the inner drill sergeant is a one-trick pony. He only yells*.

The inner drill sergeant operates through brute force, a mechanism we need more often than we care to admit. But brute force alone is inadequate,

---

* This isn't true of actual drill sergeants. I am speaking metaphorically. As a former Army officer, my experiences in boot camp, Airborne School, and my Officer Basic Course revealed that the best drill sergeants, also called drill instructors or D.I.s for short, were inspiring soldiers, experts in their field, and dedicated to the success of their charges and missions.

indeed damaging when finesse is required, much like jiggering a key in a stuck door lock.

Yelling with brute force as the sole mechanism to break our inertia is problematic because constant yelling becomes a din in which other voices become inaudible. We can't hear the piercing questions or empathic urgings from our inner coach because the barking of our inner drill sergeant is so loud.

The constant yelling soon becomes indistinguishable from constant scolding, which in turn berates with insults like "You suck, you wuss, you slug." And thus the inner drill sergeant becomes the inner critic.

Such a voice inevitably leaves us demeaned instead of emboldened at the very moment we need to be uplifted. This trajectory is particularly true in moments of gnawing anxiety or emotional pain or chronic inaction.

We can't simply will ourselves out of such states. Imagine yourself with a furrowed brow and tight fists yelling, "I won't be anxious. I won't be anxious." Or "I won't be sad. I won't be sad." Or "This time will be different. This time will be different." Good luck.

Worse still, the voice of our inner critic always projects itself outward, leaving us ever more judgmental, impatient, and blind to the struggles of other people. Our struggles, our pitfalls, and our anxieties, regardless of their source, always feel very real to us.

The "Suck it up" and "Get over it" castigations from an inner drill sergeant inevitably bring more pain not less because we end up feeling weak when they don't work.

This failure to heed isn't one of willpower
but one of hearing.

Above the din of our inner drill sergeant, it's impossible to hear the questions our inner coach might ask, such as: "What's missing for you right now? How can I support you right now? What is most important to you right now?"

Above the din we can't hear our inner coach urging us onward, cheering for us, or reminding us why this particular moment on our journey matters, thus rekindling our own desire to drive on.

And with this ember of desire rekindled it's easier to discern that second, yet oft forgotten, component of grit—passion.

Not the red-hot, uptempo, enthusiastic kind of passion, qualities impossible to summon when we are lost or toiling, but passion as commitment to something, for a worthy goal, for a purpose. It is this brand of passion married to perseverance that gets us where we want to be.

"Suck it up and move, you lazy wuss" can work well in short bursts but the sustainable advantage comes from our inner coach who counters with, "I know it's tough but you got this. C'mon, brother!"

Not only do such empathic cheers penetrate deeper, they also constitute a prerequisite element to achieving the flow state introduced in Chapter 8. Because flow requires "a sense that one's skills are adequate to cope with the challenges at hand ..." it is a place our inner critic will never know.

This flow state balance between skill and challenge constantly shifts as circumstances change: not enough skill and too much challenge brings anxiety, too much skill and not enough challenge brings boredom.

So too must we balance the voice of our inner drill sergeant: too harsh and we feel distress and shame, too soft and we succumb to impulse.

Be careful. This is a difficult balance to find. It is a tight rope walk in the pursuit of high standards, and it is why balance is one of the five power-tools in the accountability toolkit described in Chapter 2.

Moreover, when we habituate to internal criticism our sense of adequacy and capability declines. As that strength erodes, our comparative mind leaps in to find others against whom we evaluate ourselves, leaving us either "vain or bitter," as Max Herman's poem *Desiderata* warns. *(See Chapter 5, "On Not Being Good Enough.")*

But there is a third state in which our comparing mind can actually find some salvation: gratitude, if we allow it.

Gratitude can be the instant antidote to our suffering, be it a petty complaint about our workload or deep yearning for relief from pain. However, gratitude requires a quietude that our inner drill sergeant won't tolerate, but it is where our inner coach thrives.

THE NEXT STEP

1. **I often tell myself I should:** (circle one)

suck it up	drive on	deal with it
toughen up	be strong	gut it out
man up	not be a sissy, wimp, wuss, or: ______________ (insert your own word here)	

when I am...

____

____

____

(Describe struggle, activity, or emotional state; e.g. budgeting, exercising, depressed)

2. **During such moments I typically think of myself as:** (circle one)

<table>
<tr><td align="center">Your
Inner COACH Thoughts</td><td align="center">Your
Inner CRITIC Thoughts</td></tr>
<tr><td align="center">capable</td><td align="center">limited</td></tr>
<tr><td align="center">resourced</td><td align="center">outmatched</td></tr>
<tr><td align="center">matched to the task</td><td align="center">overwhelmed</td></tr>
<tr><td align="center">full of potential</td><td align="center">a phony</td></tr>
<tr><td align="center">strong</td><td align="center">a fraud</td></tr>
<tr><td align="center">smart</td><td align="center">weak</td></tr>
<tr><td align="center">disciplined</td><td align="center">dumb</td></tr>
<tr><td align="center">hopeful</td><td align="center">undisciplined</td></tr>
<tr><td align="center"></td><td align="center">pessimistic</td></tr>
</table>

3. **These thoughts typically leave me feeling:** (circle one)

<table>
<tr><td align="center">Your
Inner COACH Feelings</td><td align="center">Your
Inner CRITIC Feelings</td></tr>
<tr><td align="center">empowered</td><td align="center">disempowered</td></tr>
<tr><td align="center">healthy</td><td align="center">unhealthy</td></tr>
<tr><td align="center">inspired</td><td align="center">unmotivated</td></tr>
<tr><td align="center">ready</td><td align="center">in over my head</td></tr>
<tr><td align="center">brave</td><td align="center">scared</td></tr>
<tr><td align="center">eager</td><td align="center">hesitant</td></tr>
<tr><td align="center">excited</td><td align="center">bored</td></tr>
</table>

4. **When I feel** _______________________________,
    (insert most resonant feeling from above)
    my subsequent actions generally tend to be:
    (circle one)

Your Inner COACH Actions	Your Inner CRITIC Actions
deliberate	haphazard
decisive	slowed
powerful	inhibited
progressive	avoidant
forward	tentative
bold	halting
right	regressive
purposeful	faulty
	random

5. **When I act** _______________________________,
    (insert action from above)
    the results I generally experience are:
    (circle one)

Your Inner COACH Results	Your Inner CRITIC Results
desirable	not what I want
sustainable	unsustainable
noticeable	scant
positive	negative
uplifting	depressing
measurable	amorphous

6. **Now tie the words together and read the results from your exercise aloud.**

   When I struggle with:

   ____________________________________.

   (challenge)

   I tend to think of myself as:

   ____________________________________.

   (thoughts)

   Which usually leaves me feeling:

   ____________________________________.

   (feelings)

   Which generally causes me to:

   ____________________________________.

   (actions)

   Which invariably creates results for me that are:

   ____________________________________.

   (results)

What small adjustment can you make to find the balance between hard and soft, rough and smooth, revving or resting as you face your struggle or challenge? Write it here.

____

____

____

____

AFFIRMATION

Quietly repeat the following affirmation when you
find yourself struggling with this chapter's dilemma or
write your own using the DIY guide on page 175.

*With every burden I willingly bear, I gain strength from
the voice of my inner coach.*

MY OWN AFFIRMATION

____

____

____

____

ON GRATITUDE AND FORGIVENESS

Think of forgiveness as clearing smog from the air we breathe, and gratitude as the breath itself.

THE DILEMMA

My temper flares when I feel I'm being wronged, misunderstood, or ignored.

I get so angry at people sometimes, and it's not just strangers. Often, I lash out at the people I'm closest to.

And it's not just other people, I get really mad at myself sometimes.

Usually what I feel is disappointment or shame for some pattern of behavior that I know doesn't serve me well but I persist with.

How am I supposed to experience gratitude or forgiveness when I feel so hurt or provoked or reactive?

On a scale of 1 to 10, rate the degree to which you find this dilemma reappearing in your life. If it's more than five, reread the coaching and next steps of this chapter three more times in the next month.

| 1 | 2 | 3 | 4 | 5 | 6 | 7 | 8 | 9 | 10 |

THE TAKEAWAY

Read this chapter if it feels hard to forgive yourself for your mistakes, your shortcomings, or the hurt you inflict on others, or if you feel incredibly wronged by someone else.

You may also notice that you have a short fuse that seems to be getting shorter.

You will understand how gratitude and forgiveness work in tandem to relieve pain, soften your heart, and propel you forward.

This chapter reveals how to make gratitude and forgiveness your personal tag team, and ends with a simple exercise to help you get ready to forgive anyone for anything (including yourself), even when you don't feel anywhere near ready to do so.

It shows up in this dueling dialogue...

THE DUELING DIALOGUES

Me: Dammit, I did it again!

Critic: Yep, same old, same old.

Me: I know, I suck.

Critic: Yep, total fail.

COACH: At what?

Me: Doing what I said I'd do today
to grow my business.

Critic: You've been not doing that for
months, hell, years.

COACH: Not growing his business? What are you
talking about? He's built something good.

Critic: Not doing enough of what he said he'd
do to make it better. Today it was make the
calls. Last week it was drip marketing. Last
month it was automation. Last year it was
delegation. I'm sick of it.

Me: I know. And I keep promising myself it'll be
different this day, this week. I just keep repeating

the same patterns of avoidance or half-starts, and then beating myself up for it.

COACH: Ouch.

Critic: Damn right, ouch. It should sting.

COACH: Why?

Critic: So we can whip his ass into shape.

COACH: You've been doing that quite a bit. How about we try something new?

Me: I've tried everything: planners, lists, sticks, carrots, discipline days, focus days, buddy systems, goal setting, and outsourcing, you name it. I make progress but then fall back.

COACH: How about forgiveness?

Critic: No way! You're gonna give him permission for this pattern?

COACH: You believe that the problem is your pattern of behavior. But you haven't unearthed why it persists or dealt with the aftermath.

Me: Do you mean the impact on my business? I know it's bad.

COACH: No, not especially. I mean the impact on other people and your sense of self. You feel tense, you're angry, hurt, and disappointed. Besides feeling crappy about yourself and slowing your business, what else happens?

Me: Nothing. It's just internal strife: mixed up, fed up, torn up.

Critic: Ha! Until some random moment when his daughter shows up late or his wife mentions some undone chore. Then he lashes out and blames them, instead of looking at his own behavior.

COACH: I understand that. It's easy to do when you haven't processed your own experience enough to understand it.

Critic: Process schmocess, that's lame.

COACH: No, it's logical, even predictable when you're in a dysfunctional loop. If you don't understand it, you'll keep cycling in it.

Me: What does that have to do with forgiveness?

COACH: Forgiveness gives you a fresh start. If you want to move from mixed up anger and blame and projection onto others you've got to develop self compassion, which can only come from self-understanding, which you need to forgive yourself.

Critic: Forgive, my ass! There's no excuse.

COACH: We're not excusing the behavior, we're understanding it. Listen! There's your unwanted behavior, then sadness or anger about the behavior, then hurt or shame beneath that, which leads to guilt or remorse, and then back to earnest but hollow promises to change; all the while never getting to the roots of what ails you. Get to the root, and you can break the cycle.

Critic: But he still has to take responsibility for his actions and for the damage he's done.

COACH: Absolutely! Responsibility first, and then accountabilities. Let's own the damage, then we can unpack it.

Me: What do you mean own it?

COACH: I mean there's no one else to blame, it's on you to change, and you must acknowledge the hurt you caused. That's ownership!

Me: I can take ownership.

COACH: I can forgive you.

THE COACHING

I struggle with apologizing—that solo act of contrition that leads me to face my shame. Not only do I prefer to avoid it, I also have so damn many offenses that warrant forgiveness, I fear I've cheapened the act of seeking it—from myself or from other people.

Be they self-inflicted wounds or damage to others, be they petty offenses or potent ones, I often struggle with a slew of overlapping, interweaving, contradictory, and fluctuating emotions related to forgiveness.

Selling well and serving well can't be done sustainably when we are tied in emotional knots because we can't bring our full selves to the game. When you try to *fake it till you make it* in this circumstance, the destination is always deeper strife, never relief.

In Chapter 1, "On Anxiety," I describe how forgiveness and gratitude align like the rear and front sights on a rifle when we take aim at relieving our anxiety. But it's not just anxiety we can target, it's all manner of fist-clenching, chest-tightening, brow-furrowing distress.

By themselves, forgiveness and gratitude are potent medicines to soothe the critic's savage soul; often, they are sufficient in and of themselves to advance wellness. Combined, however, they amplify the voice of our inner coach. Forgiveness opens fresh space that gratitude permits us to occupy.

I have experienced the power of this combination many times. One simple but illustrative instance was during a long walk home when I was tired, hungry, and sore after a full day of physical exertion and not enough calories. I was grumpy and spent.

Arriving at the doorstep of my rented apartment in the small Spanish town where I was living, I suddenly remembered my commitment to meet a local farmer at his smallholding to retrieve my weekly allotment. Not a big deal—except that it was a three-mile, round-trip walk. No bike, no car, no cab.

In that moment, when I had been grouchy and exhausted, I suddenly became angry and resentful to boot because I knew I had to make the trip. A promise is a promise after all.

As I groused and grumbled and walked, a soothing voice popped into my head completely affirming my feelings. This was the voice of self compassion— that necessary precursor to forgiveness—which immediately felt comforting. "Of course you don't want to do this, Sheldon. You are exhausted and it is a long walk and you deserve a rest."

In that same instance it occurred to me how lucky I was to be on my way to collecting fresh, organic veggies grown by a local farmer. I imagined him laboring with love.

I thought of impoverished children who walk miles not only for food but for water, and then felt deep gratitude that I had both. I grew grateful for the money in my pocket, the strength of my body, and the beauty of my surroundings.

And just as quickly my mood switched from bitter to ebullient. By forgiving my foul temper, my typical "suck it up and deal" approach melted into the warmth of gratitude.

Think of forgiveness as clearing smog from the air we breathe, and gratitude as the breath itself. From this perspective we can inhale what our inner coach urges instead of what our critic spews.

Take, for example, your justifiable rage at anyone who has insulted, hurt, or otherwise wronged you, up close or even from afar. While we are at it, take the self-loathing you pour into your heart for personal lapses in judgment, failures of will, mistakes, or defeats.

Forgive all that? Hell no! The wound is too deep, the pain is too fresh. To forgive is to capitulate and gratitude is irrelevant. If I forgive, my tormentor gets off scot-free. Where is the justice? Where are the standards? Where is the accountability?!

Pause those questions for now and ask instead, "What happens when I hold on to a grievance? How does it make me feel to stew in the insult, injury, or personal failing?"

Torn.

Torn as in not whole. Torn from grace, from peace, from the essence of who we are.

Archbishop Desmond Tutu, anti-apartheid and human-rights activist, and leader of South Africa's Truth and Reconciliation Commission, wrote a beautiful book with his daughter, Mpho, called *The Book of Forgiving*. In it he describes how all acts of forgiveness, large or small, move us closer to wholeness, to our essential nature.

He writes, and I believe, that our inherent nature is goodness, that no one is born cruel or a criminal, or a constant critic but that we are each born whole and good. By stewing in an unwillingness to forgive ourselves or others, we tear the fabric of our wholeness, we break the bonds of our shared humanity. Forgiveness binds it afresh.

Moreover, without forgiveness, we remain tethered to the person who harmed us or to our lesser self. We are held by chains of bitterness and blame. We can't elevate because we remain shackled to our distress. Forgiveness is liberating. But it's damn hard.

Gratitude, on the other hand, is an easy place to find. What's tricky is staying put, especially when we've been wronged by an outer or an inner tormentor hauling us away to the land of accusation and complaint.

On a vacation, at a party, in a groove, or over a sumptuous meal, it's easy to be grateful. But that's not when we need the anchor. We need it during surges of blame or shame. Gratitude reveals what is enough rather than what is lacking.

It also, in a beautiful symbiosis, uncorks the same fount of neurochemicals that are released when we give. Serotonin and dopamine be praised! *(See Chapter 7, "On The Keys To Success.")*

Gratitude says to your heart and mind, "Looky here, in this present moment right now, here is a blessing, this is good."

Forgiveness makes a similar call. It says, "You don't need to hold on to that which has given you pain or difficulty. It's a heavy burden you can drop."

But I sometimes turn a deaf ear to both. When I'm guilty of a persistent yet petty offense, say, criticizing my wife for a purchase, myself for a squandered day, or my daughter for her messy room, I'm almost always replaying an old narrative that I refuse to replace. Or worse still, I'm projecting onto others fears or failures of my own. In either case, forgiveness and gratitude are absent.

> *"This forgiveness-gratitude loop is all fine and dandy," you may say, "but this person is [or I am] a repeat offender, the damage is deep, the stakes are high, the wound is mortal. Forget forgiveness and gratitude! I want recompense."*

Don't we all.

Big pain compounds the difficulty by orders of magnitude but the formula still works. I know this because I've been both the benefactor and beneficiary at a grand scale.

If Holocaust survivor Victor Frankl and Desmond Tutu can find it in their hearts to forgive the unimaginable horrors they endured, and live in gratitude, I can, too.

Gratitude magically feeds upon itself to help us get more of what we want at the precise moment that forgiveness opens the door to receive it. But there is no screaming at the door to be heard, only a soft-spoken coach bearing daily gifts.

"And if we do not accept these gifts," as Ralph Waldo Emerson warns, "they are carried as silently away." To live more frequently in states of gratitude and forgiveness is to transform the voice of your inner critic into your championship coach.

Perhaps that's why the most famous prayer in all of Christianity expresses gratitude for our daily bread and asks God to "forgive us our trespasses, as we forgive those who trespass against us."

THE NEXT STEP

— FORGIVENESS —

When you are really angry at yourself or at someone else, and are not at all interested in forgiveness, offer up this portion of the "Prayer Before the Prayer" found in *The Book of Forgiving*, by Desmond Tutu and Mpho Tutu:

"I want to be willing to forgive
But dare not ask for the will to forgive
In case you give it to me
And I am not yet ready
I am not yet ready for my heart to soften
I am not yet ready to be vulnerable again
Not yet ready to see that there is humanity in
my tormentor's eyes
Or that the one who hurt me may also have cried
I am not yet ready for the journey
I am not yet interested in the path
I am at the prayer before the prayer of forgiveness
Grant me the will to want to forgive
Grant it to me not yet but soon"

—GRATITUDE—

I attempted this simple, three-part gratitude practice daily, immediately upon waking, for a year. I even tracked my progress with tick-marks on a calendar. After a few months, the practice became almost automatic. Now, I awaken most days with all manner of simple blessings flooding my consciousness.

1. Think about yourself and write one thing that you love about yourself.

   ____

2. Think about where you live and write one thing that is beautiful.

   ____

3. Think about a person you love and write one thing that you cherish about them.

   ____

4. Now tie all three objects together and say them aloud in a single sentence beginning with the words, I feel deep gratitude for ...

   ____

   ____

   ____

   ____

5. Repeat the sentence slowly, with your eyes closed. Breathe deeply and put a faint smile on your face as you say the words.

AFFIRMATION

Quietly repeat the following affirmation when you find yourself struggling with this chapter's dilemma or write your own using the DIY guide on page 175.

As I want to be forgiven, so will I forgive.

I welcome the gifts of my miraculous body, an abundant earth,

precious people and the will to nurture all.

MY OWN AFFIRMATION

____

____

____

____

CHAPTER ∞

DIY RULES TO CREATE SELF-AFFIRMATIONS

Affirmations can sound like cheesy schlock. They can also soothe the savage beast.

Every chapter ends with an affirmation as the last action step. Use the one provided or create your own using these three rules as a Do It Yourself (DIY) guide.

A vast body of clinical research confirms that self-affirmations are an effective tonic, but only if you act as if the affirmations are true. Which, of course, they are.

RULE ONE

Rote recitations won't work. Effective affirmations aren't rah-rah, pump me up, lovely delusions in the face of doubt or despair. They are positively stated, present-tense truths grounded in what you value and know about yourself.

For example:

- Not: "I know how to attract abundance and I can make all the money I desire" if you are struggling with money and self-doubt.

- But: "I know abundance surrounds me and I am capable of gathering more," which is more believable to your struggling self.

RULE TWO

Your present-tense, credible, and believable affirmation must also be stated positively using "I" statements.

For example:

- Not: "I will avoid wasting time on prospects who don't value my services," which is negative.

- But: "I believe my territory is full of prospects I know I can serve and I eagerly seek them out."

RULE THREE

Experiment. Like a radio dial, tune your words until you get a clear signal.

The difference between static and music on a radio is like the difference between cheesiness and resonance with an affirmation: a tiny adjustment may be all it takes.

Try a quick experiment now.

1. Call to mind a current struggle, worry, pain, fear, or doubt. State it.

2. Without pondering, point your finger to any of the following "I" statements:

   I am…   I can…   I choose…   I accept…

   I release…   I welcome…   I invite…   I trust…

   I believe…   I have…   I know…   I love…

3. Test ways to complete the sentence with uplifting and reassuring language that rings true and speaks to your struggle.

   Remember, aspirational, action-oriented, positive, and believable are key. Get to it!

ACKNOWLEDGEMENTS

The Nicene Creed begins, "I believe in one God, the Father, the Almighty, maker of heaven and earth, of all that is seen and unseen." But that triggers folk who get hung up on words like, God, Father, and heaven. Not me. I appreciate the poetry of Source in that prayer and feel grateful as I consider how this book came to be. I'm also grateful to many humans.

My Dad, who always full of witticisms, also brings great depth, strong counsel and unflagging support. And my Mom, God rest her soul, the grammarian, the thespian, and contrarian.

My loving brother, Bond, who turned an early draft of this book from an overreaching sermon into a useful path to growth.

My courageous, fierce and tender wife, Judy Goldman whose insights as a clinical psychologist permeate every page.

My daughters, Isabel and Julia, who helped me keep things real.

My patient editor, Beth Ann Dailey, whose constant refrain, "What are you trying to say?" shaped each chapter of this book.

My dear friend and talented designer, Seth Gregory, a cheerleader who transformed my artistic vision into this beautiful and useful field guide.

My expert book publishing consultant, Kimberly Martin of Jera Publishing who, like a humble sherpa, guided me to the summit and back.

And to my band of brothers called Vaderaid who are a bunch of badass, hard charging, highly accomplished athletes, adventurers, professionals and family men with whom I navigate the constant interplay of light and dark.

EPILOGUE

"Oh, sweetie, that's a terrible way to talk to yourself."
Such was the tender reminder from my wife as I was criticizing my softening muscles and growing paunch while in the final stages of completing this book.
I'm such a hypocrite.

No. Such a human.

I think I'll go re-read that passage about practice.

SPECIAL OFFER

Visit AnxiousSalesman.com for worksheet downloads and our free implementation webinar:

How to transform your inner critic into a championship coach to help you sell like never before.

(Especially if you are sick of rah-rah mindset hype, and alpha-male be-a-closer BS!)

AnxiousSalesman.com